ISAAC GRIJALVA

6 1/2 Days In The City

First edition

ISBN (paperback): 9798994059234
ISBN (hardcover): 9798994059241

Editing by Mary Whitney

This book was professionally typeset on Reedsy.
Find out more at reedsy.com

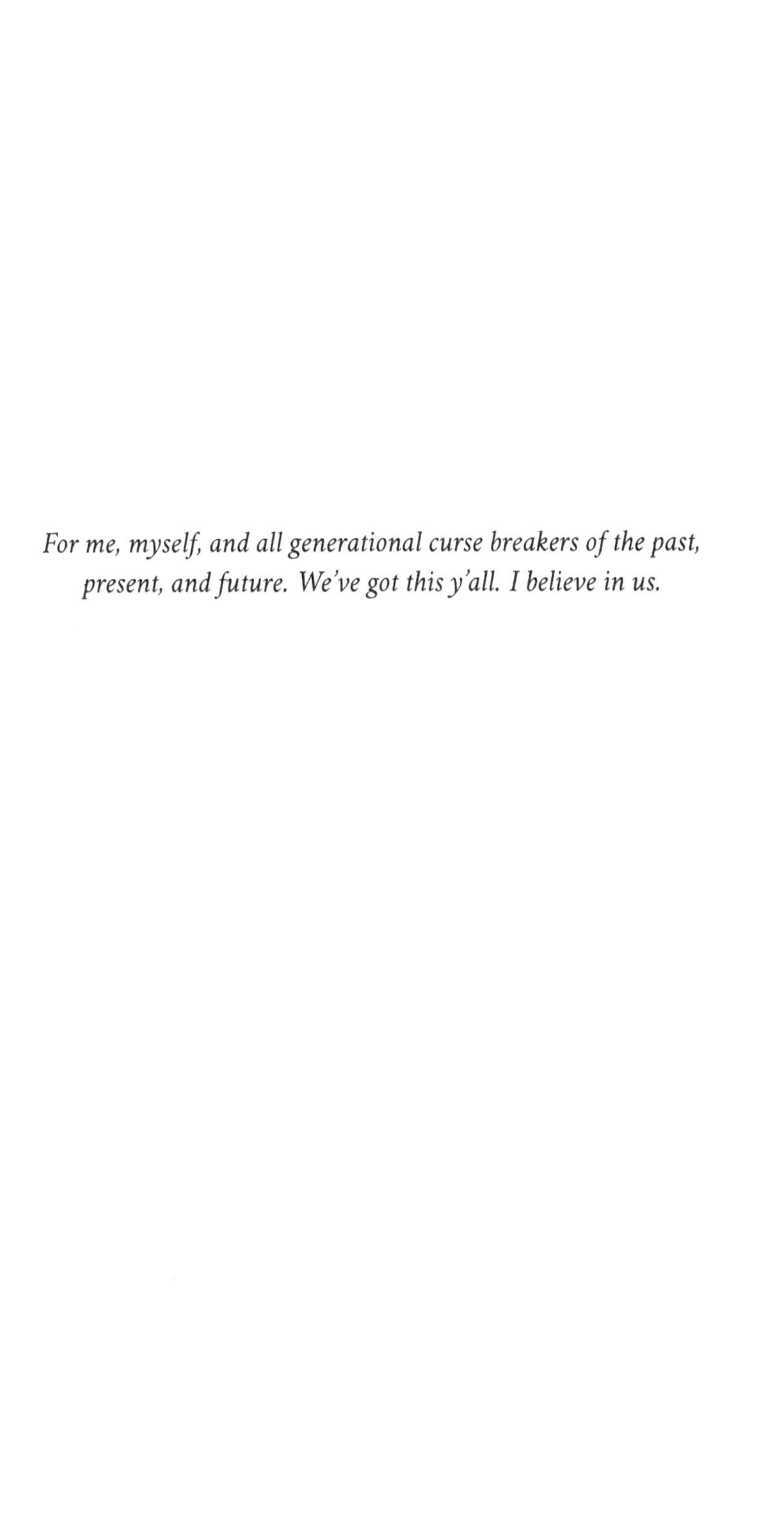

For me, myself, and all generational curse breakers of the past, present, and future. We've got this y'all. I believe in us.

Contents

Foreword — ii
Acknowledgments — iii
6 1/2 Days In The City — 1
About the Author — 156

Foreword

CONTENT WARNING: This novel contains the following

- graphic sexual content
- bisexual sexual behaviors
- ethical non-monogamous sex acts
- mental health awareness
- psychiatric crisis
- mentions of sexual assault (off page)
- mentions of childhood neglect (off page)
- generational trauma

If you or anyone else you know is struggling with thoughts of harming yourself or others, please ask for help. Know that you aren't alone and there is light at the end of the tunnel.

Acknowledgments

First and foremost, I want to express how absolutely grateful I am to everyone who made this book possible to begin with. Special thank you to my editing team and cover designers. Thank you to my real life Xiomara, who gave me the idea for the book in the first place. Thank you for supporting me in every endeavor of my life from the personal, to the academic, social, and professional. Thank you to my friends who read the earliest versions of this book and gave me their feedback to make this story what it is now. Thank you so much to my family, Mom and Dad, Cris and the baby, and all my cousins who've brought love, light, and magic to my life in ways I cannot begin to describe. Of course, thank you so much to my real life Asia and Red who inspired the friendship and elements of found family in this book. You have both been so grounding and supportive in everything I've done since we were 15 years old. Thank you to my grandmother, Nina, who read some of my earliest works from the Big Time Rush Christmas Carol (James was Scrooge) to the Halloween story that I wrote with Big Time Rush, the Jonas Brothers, and members of the iCarly cast. Last, but certainly not least, a *special special* thanks to April and Tommy Mouton. Thank you so much for believing in my earliest manuscripts and introducing me to the self-publishing world at the age of 13 years old. My writing journey would have likely ended if not for you two.

6 1/2 Days In The City

October 28th, 2025, 2 Days Before The City

Code Blue, Emergency Room, Room 3. Code Blue, Emergency Room, Room 3. The words rang out through the hospital as my partner and I wheeled in the dead patient. The Cal-Fire EMT was straddling her as he did compressions. The ER was a flurry of nurses, running to prep the bed to run this code. The doctor held her arm out to clear a way and let us enter the room.

As the nurses and my EMTs transferred the patient to the hospital bed, I stood off to the side with the doctor to give her the report. The patient wasn't this bad when we first arrived on scene. She was semi-conscious. The call had come in as simply "grandma's not acting right." We got her hooked up to the monitor, loaded her up, and started driving. Halfway through the ride, she stopped breathing. The Cal-Fire EMT confirmed she didn't have a carotid pulse. He compressed. My partner pulled over and hopped into the back to prep an *i-Gel* and bag valve mask to start bagging the patient as I applied the AED. We shocked the shockable rhythm after the first round of compressions. I drilled into the patient's tibia to push the epinephrine after the next round when no shock was advised. We got pulses back in the pulse check. We contacted base hospital. The patient qualified for transport after the pulses held for five minutes. Lights and sirens were toned up. The Cal-Fire EMT bagged on the way. We lost the pulses just as we were pulling in. The Cal-Fire EMT straddled the patient as my partner and I pulled her out.

Patient care had been transferred. I was free to go. Despite the adrenaline dump, I left the room feeling exhausted.

"Lord, have mercy," I muttered, blowing out a huge breath. My head was still spinning from the call.

A few other crews were waiting in the halls for room placement. I nodded a greeting to them and knuckle-touched the ones that I went to school with.

The blast of cold air felt almost rejuvenating as I walked outside. I sat down on one of the benches to write my patient care report. My EMT came out with the gurney to decontaminate it. The Cal-Fire EMT was behind him, yapping to anyone around that would listen to how cool the call that we just ran was.

Once it was time to go, I heaved a huge sigh as we got into the ambulance. My partner cleared us with Dispatch. They cleared us to get gas and return to the station. We were finally done for the night. Thank fucking *GOD*. My partner and I were ran to shit all day for four days straight. My *bones* were tired.

I rested my head against the cold window, wishing that I could sleep on the way. My mind was too occupied with everything going on. It wasn't just the call. Yes, I was exhausted, but I was also anxious to get out of Merced. In two days, I was going to fly to New York City to see my best friends from high school, Asia and Red. One week of paid vacation time to get away from all this chaos going on. One last shebang before I started school again.

Once we got back to the station, we cleared out of the ambulance, grabbed our bags and let our cleaning and restocking crew take over. They were bumping *corridos* on those old school boom boxes and dancing together. I smirked and shook my head at them as I walked away to check in the narcotics that were onboard.

While punching in the codes on the little vials, I heard the door to my rear left creak open.

"You back for the night?" It was one of the supervisors, Ventura. He was the man who'd trained and cleared me to be both an EMT and a Paramedic. He's also the man who wrote me the letter of recommendation that helped get me into my post-baccalaureate program, which would help me through the med school application process. "We need to speak for a second."

I looked over my shoulder. It was nice to see him. However, something told me that it wasn't just to catch up. "Yeah. I'll be right there."

The supervisor's office was quite stuffy, with a lot of desks scattered around with chairs around them. His was in a far corner. I took my uniform jacket off as I approached him, feeling the hot air trapped inside lift and enjoying the cooling sensation that it left behind.

His back was still turned to me, his fingers clacking on his keyboard as I pulled the chair out and sat. Ventura swiveled his chair around and put his glasses up into the front of his thinning hair.

"Alright, Mancía," he started, placing his elbows on the table, balling his fists and resting his chin on them. "What's going on?"

I cocked my head at him and raised an eyebrow. "Uhm–"

"C'mon…" he coaxed, giving me a look and rolling his hand to get me to speak. "Anything going on at home? Having a hard time dealing with the call volume, call type, anything like that?"

I stared at him, as neutral as I could. *Well,* I thought, *now that you ask. My parents' health is deteriorating slowly but surely. My 10-year-old dog is getting old and arthritic. My mother (despite how much I love her) has been driving my father crazy at home now that she has been forced into retirement after her work injury. There's a tiny voice in my head that, despite my best friends never giving me an inkling of rejection or repugnance, keeps telling me that they actually hate me. That I'm a burden to them and that my visits to New York City bug them because I'm a horrible guest–*

I shook my head, partly to say no and partly to stop the

inundation of thought. "Nothing too out of the ordinary." I technically wasn't lying to him. He bit his thumb while looking at me. "Did I do something wrong?"

He shook his head. "No," he told me. It felt like his eyes peered into my soul. He knew I wasn't telling the truth. "I'm not going to twist your arm into telling me anything that you aren't comfortable with–" I felt bad not being comfortable with him. I've known the man for years. I came to him after bad breakups, bad calls, when my parents or younger brother irritated me, and when I felt homesick for the Bay Area. He was my mentor and my friend. He was everything that I wanted to be as a medic–from operations, to patient care, to documentation. "But I've noticed… a *downward* trend in the way that you've been doing things around here."

That stung a little.

"I can see it in your reports… in your assessments…" He shook his head sadly. "You're not a bad medic, Cameron." He rubbed his hands together while his facial expressions softened. "You're a damn good one."

My lip turned up in a small smile. "I learned from the best."

He huffed a laugh. "I just don't want you to… *get complacent*. I haven't heard anything about your patient care that's concerning 'cause that's still top notch." He smiled at me as I raised my hands in a cocky gesture. "But I need to see improvements before it starts doing so."

I swallowed the lump that had been forming in my throat, doing my best not to let myself get teary-eyed. That's the last thing I ever wanted. "Right," my voice broke. "I know."

He sighed deeply. I knew he hated having to put on the supervisor hat. He wiped his face with one hand. "I understand that you're about to go on vacation?"

"Yes," I sighed, closing my eyes briefly. I felt the giddy nerves course through me. "Friends of mine from high school live out in New York, so I'm going out to see them for the week."

"Good!" Ventura cheered, clasping his hands together. "It'll be good for you. Hopefully, that's what you need, huh? A nice little escape from all the chaos?"

I nodded, taking another deep breath and letting it out. The day–the week, really–had done its number on me.

"When are you starting school again?" he asked. "You'll be going part-time here to prioritize that, right?"

I nodded, feeling the good nerves. I had to go back to school. I wasn't supposed to be a medic for this long. I told him when I started. "Finally."

Someone else walked in, and we shook hands as a formal goodbye.

I walked out into the pitch black parking lot. We got held over quite a bit. It was almost 5 am. We were supposed to be off at

2. I got into my car, gripped the steering wheel and rested my forehead on the leather. *I have to get out of here*, I thought to myself.

*****

Not even 5 hours later, I was up and in my parents' kitchen, making breakfast. I was wearing basketball shorts and a tank top, holding my 9-month-old niece in one arm under her butt while she clung to me with one hand. My parents called me that morning, asking me to come over and make breakfast for them, my brother Luke, and the baby.

My niece, Aurora, looked down intently at the scrambled eggs as they cooked on the stove. She was wearing a pink onesie and had her pacifier in her mouth.

I felt a little better than I did just a few hours ago, especially since Aurora and Luke were here.

"Such a pretty girl, huh, mama?" I cooed. I kissed her forehead. She smiled with her pacifier in her mouth, almost dropping it. I looked down and saw the family dog, Bailey, sitting there by the sink, looking up at me expectantly. She's a black chihuahua-terrier mutt who's *fat*. Her head was tilted to the side. Her tail wagged a little, brushing the floor with each swipe. She wasn't just hungry. She was jealous. "You're my pretty girl too, *princesa.*"

While cooking, I started sorting through the logistics of what I'd be doing with Asia and Red once I got into town. We've known each other since our sophomore year of high school, when I still lived in San Jose. We've kept in touch after all these years, after moving to the Valley. The two of them moved out to New York when Asia started her Master's in something fancy that I can never remember over at Columbia. Since Red worked a remote position, it just made sense for him to join her. I visited them earlier this year, back in April. That was when they lived off Broadway, closer to the university. Now, they live in Central Harlem.

Last time I came over, Red was only there for the last two days of my stay because his job sometimes required in-person meetings back in the Bay Area. This time, he was going to be there the whole time. So I was excited to take him to the Bronx Zoo and Coney Island—highlights of the trip last time. Maybe watch a movie or two and catch a Broadway show.

Then, of course, there were going to be what I liked to call my *side quests.* Eight million people in the city, and I knew that at least one of them wanted to fuck me. I had no idea what his real name was. He never told me. I saved him in my contacts as *Balkan Man* because he told me he was from the Balkans. There were going to be other side quests, of course. Him for sure, though.

"What time are you leaving for New York tomorrow?" Luke asked, standing in the doorway from the living room to the kitchen.

"Around eight," I told him, flipping the eggs with one hand. "I want to get there early just in case TSA has fucked delays because of the shutdown."

"Mmm," he grunted, reaching for the baby as she started getting fussy and calling for him. "Come here, baby. She want Dada?"

"Did you need anything?" I offered. "I can do it before I go. Still got the whole day after laundry gets done."

"Nah," he yawned, holding the baby close to his chest. "We'll figure it out."

I was about to insist when our dad called him and the baby into the living room.

When I sat down to finally eat, I got a text message from my friend, Xiomara. She and I had gotten quite close over the last 5-6 months since we started talking. We matched on the dating/hook-up app, *F That*. After several instances of going days without talking to each other, I decided to take our communication a little more seriously. I was initially very drawn to her because she was a Master's student who worked as a guidance counselor at one of the high schools in San Jose. I loved having a good excuse to go back home, so I went out to see her a lot. She'd do the same. We decided to be friends pretty quickly after meeting. Meeting her, I didn't feel drawn to her in the way that I thought I would be. Funny enough, she was ready to jump my bones the first time that we met. She told me she felt silly for asking and getting rejected because she'd shaved for me and everything. She was hilarious in that way. Over the last few months, I'd say we got pretty close. I was very comfortable around her and considered her a close friend. Not Asia and Red close. But more than a friend that I only check on occasionally.

I told her I was spending time with family and that I would talk to her later. She apologized for imposing on family time. I told her she was fine. Then I put my phone away.

We put the baby in her bouncer on wheels with gadgets, rattles, and colored lights. She looked up expectantly at my brother before she started to swat at different pieces with one hand, with the other hand in her mouth.

Luke got up and started playing with the baby. "Come on, baby! We jumping! Jumping, jumping, jumping!" He didn't really jump. He pushed up onto his tippy toes after shooting up from a slight knee bend. She started laughing at him and started repeating what he was doing. My heart swelled and melted. I loved it when she did that. It was the cutest thing ever. My parents and I took a few pictures and videos of her. She was such a photogenic baby. She knew just when to look at the camera. Even in candid shots, it almost looked like she knew the camera was on her. She would point, wiggle her limbs around in excitement, or look up with her huge eyes at whoever's lap she was in.

I loved having little moments like this with them. As much as my parents could get on my nerves, I loved them. I missed living with them, too. The apartment was quiet, and it was nice living on my own. I just felt bad for leaving them on their own sometimes. Mom was forced to retire from work because of a work injury after she got hit by a car in the parking lot and broke her hip. Now she walked with a permanent limp. Dad had been out of work for over a decade after his back went out. He had a heart attack this year. His health had been in the dumps for a while now, but that's what really scared us. They had to vacate the house they had been renting for decades. Now they lived in this small, rent-controlled apartment just down the street from where I live.

As we sat watching some random medical comedy show on *Peacock*, Luke started getting ready to leave with the baby. I got a little emotional watching him go. Of everyone in the family, I knew that I missed my brother the most. We hung out a lot at my place after I finally moved out, when my union raise at work kicked in. Then he moved to college, and his absence left a massive hole in my parents' house. Now that he had the baby, he was back. He just wasn't around anymore. He had his own place with his girlfriend, Daniela.

I started getting ready, too. I might love and miss my parents, but there was a reason why I moved out when I did. They're very overbearing. It felt weird and incredibly forced.

"Leaving so soon, baby?" my mom asked me as I stood up. She was sitting next to my dad with her head on his shoulder.

Before I could even look at her and answer, my dad said, "You know Cameron doesn't like hanging out with us anymore. Too good for us now."

My mom slapped his arm and shot him a look. I knew that he was trying to make a joke. In that moment, it seemed rich. It wasn't that my parents weren't there for us when we were younger; they were. It just didn't feel like they knew us. We were their kids. They were our parents. It was normal when we were kids. Now that I'm older, it's shitty to have emotionally unavailable parents.

I bit my tongue and scoffed, pointing a finger at him. "I'm gonna go now."

"Cameron, wait!" they shouted after me.

"Nope!" I shouted back, slamming the screen door as I left.

I heaved a huge sigh of relief now that I was out. *Just one more day Cameron*, I told myself.

October 29th, 2025, 1 Day Before The City

Since my flight was leaving just before 1 pm, I was up at 7. My bag was packed by 7:30. I made sure I had everything, of course. The very first thing I packed was my Halloween costume. I was going to be the Joker and was really looking forward to it. I didn't give much thought to the other outfits that I selected. As long as I had the basics, I was satisfied.

I stuffed my face quickly with some granola bars. I grabbed an energy drink from the fridge just in case. The last thing that I wanted to do was fall asleep at the wheel. I'd almost done it, too. Driving back from my pediatric clinical hours at Valley Children's a few years ago, sleep-deprived, after a 12 hr 7 am to 7 pm shift. I caught myself nodding off just before having to swerve away from the railing as the road curved.

I looked around the dark apartment for my sneakers. Once I found them, I slipped into my sneakers, not caring if the heels were folding. I was trying to get the hell out of there. I was trying to get to New York.

I drove to San Jose listening mainly to Taylor Swift, Big Time Rush, Maluma, Green Day, and the Jonas Brothers. I was so excited to get the hell out of Merced that I didn't need the energy drink. Good thing, too, because without a decent meal, the caffeine would make me shit.

I got to the parking garage, where I could leave my car for just $8/night, 2.5 hrs before boarding was to start. Almost like she had a 6th sense, Xiomara started calling me the second I parked and went for my bags in the back seat.

"Hey," I answered. "I just got to San Jose. I'm taking the bags out of the car."

"Okaaaayyyyy," she replied. "Look at you, finally acting Type A." I rolled my eyes and huffed a laugh. "You didn't forget anything, did you?"

"No, Xiomara," I told her, throwing the duffel over my shoulder and locking the car.

She snickered. "Okay, Cameron." I heard her take a bite of something. "I'm just asking."

She was talking about something that her brother was doing to annoy her as I sat and laid everything out on the bench where I would wait for the shuttle to take us to SJC. Duffel bag. Carry on. Phone. Retainer case in my right shorts pocket. My wa-

I squeezed my left thigh *HARD*. MY WALLET. I turned out both pockets while Xiomara kept talking. Nothing. I knew it wasn't in either bag.

My heart sank. My breathing hitched. My wallet was in my work pants. My *wallet...* with my credit cards, debit cards, and most importantly, *MY REAL ID CARD REQUIRED TO CHECK MY BAG IN AND PASS TSA.*

"Hello?" Xiomara called out. "Are you still there?"

"Yeah," I panted, already halfway back to the car to make sure it wasn't on the floor or in the cupholder or in the console in between the front two seats. "Xiomara, I left my stupid fucking wallet in Merced!"

She went silent for a bit. "You're fucking kid-"

"No! I'm not!" I snapped. "FUCK!" I got a few stares from people nearby. I couldn't fucking believe this. How the fuck did I forget the MOST IMPORTANT thing I needed for this goddamn vacation? "Hey, I'm gonna let you go. I'm gonna call my brother to bring it to me. If he leaves in the next half hour, he'll get here fast enough."

I didn't even wait for her to agree to hang up. The phone rang for what felt like an eternity. My brother was asleep. I was afraid he wasn't gonna answer, let alone want to drive over 2 hrs to get here. Thank fucking God, he agreed. We were going to meet in Livermore, so he didn't have to drive through Pacheco Pass when he was tired.

Hanging up with Luke, Xiomara was already sending me screenshots of other available flights with my airline. There were two left tonight. One was leaving at 8:15 pm, stopping in Vegas and then Chicago, which would get me into La Guardia in Queens around 1 pm tomorrow. The next left 20 minutes later, stopped in the same places, and would get me into La Guardia at precisely 9 am. Thankfully, it was free to make the switch.

I almost started crying. I didn't know if it was from frustration or relief. I didn't want to look childish at the parking garage.

I explained my situation to the men at the check-in and told them I'd be back later tonight to drop off the car. I now had several hours of free time. I was *so* fucking relieved. I don't know what the fuck I would've done if I had gotten stuck out here and hadn't been able to switch the flight times. I huffed a laugh at the thought. I would've cried like a big fucking baby, that's for sure. I found some street parking so I could sit and think about what I wanted to do. It was the middle of the workday, so many of my family members and friends from high school were probably at work.

Nobody was answering, so I just went to the mall on my own. My aunt runs her own business on the first floor of Eastridge. I make jokes that she runs it like a sweatshop, and she always laughs. I wanted to see her.

When I got there, I walked in and asked for her by name. She rounded the corner, and then my aunt came out wearing her work smock and blue jeans, her hair done up in a messy bun that still looked put together.

"Well, what's up?!" she greeted. Her arms were open wide to hug me. "How you been?"

She introduced me to the new hires during their orientation. Some were working with clients. Others were hanging up mannequins. Her coworkers were really friendly.

"This is Cameron," my aunt introduced. "The paramedic. The one I'm always bragging about." She put a hand to the corner of her mouth and stage whispered. "Gonna be a doctor someday, so tell your nieces and nephews."

I scoffed a laugh. Everyone thought she was a hoot. I left the room with a few "nice to meet you, sweetie"s. She showed me around a little more.

We walked around the store while she tidied up the little things that were out of place and talked about Luke and Aurora. I showed her pictures of the baby and how cute she was. I told her that he was doing better in school nowadays. I told her that he was training to run in the Olympics in three years. It was all very overwhelming. Not only was I proud of him, but I also loved him so much. The little boy who used to run around the hallways in my oversized clothes because he wanted to be just like me is a grown ass man now.

A little after noon, we started making our way back upstairs to the parking lot.

The drive back to Luke was really fast, especially since I had to pee really badly. He called me just before I got into town to tell him I was getting close. He told me to meet him at McDonald's. I pulled into the parking lot and called him to let him know I was there and to order whatever he wanted.

After relieving myself, we sat at a window seat with ample sunlight once he grabbed his food. He handed me my wallet back.

"Thank you so much for coming," I told him, slumping down into the seat. I put my face into my hands and rubbed it. "You have no idea how much of a lifesaver you are."

"Mm." His mouth was full. "It's all good. I know you'd have done the same for me."

Of course I would have. "How's the baby doing?"

"Good, still waking us up hella early." He snickered, holding his burger with two hands the way I'd shown him when we were little. "She was putting her hands all up in my face this morning. Tryna pull off my bonnet and shit."

I giggled at the thought. "She's so cute."

We sat in silence for a second while he ate.

I started thinking about when I took him to New Mexico three years prior. It was spring break, and our grandmother lived in a small retirement town called Rio Rancho. We went for the weekend to see her for Easter and then left for Albuquerque, where we stayed in an Airbnb. We had a lot of fun out there. We went to a few museums, the zoo, the bio park, the Breaking Bad store, and the theaters. We were going to go to Santa Fe, but we ended up at the wrong train station for the train up there. By the time the next train was supposed to come into town, we'd only have like 45 minutes to an hour to see anything. It was everything I'd ever hoped for in a vacation with him. At the end of the week, we were lying on my twin bed in my room after getting back and being exhausted from travel, and he rolled over and threw his arm around me. He told me how much fun he had with me.

My brother burped loudly into his mouth. "Excuse me." He patted his chest and cleared his throat aggressively. "Girl, goddamn!"

Soon after that, he was ready to leave. I walked with him to his car.

"I love you," I told him, stepping away after we hugged. "I'm gonna send you some money right now."

"Okay, love you."

We parted ways.

Before heading back, I grabbed gas. On the way to San Jose, I got a call from Xiomara. She wanted to drive up from the south side and get food with me at the mall.

We met up at Eastridge and grabbed some Subway. The meal of the day was the meatball marinara, so we got that and shared it.

"Do you like my shirt?" she asked, gesturing to it with one hand like someone showing off merchandise on TV.

"I dooooo," I complimented. I smirked. "It really accentuates your tits."

She scoffed and let out a single laugh. "I know." She put a hand under her chin, grinned widely and looked up.

I shook my head at her. "And you call me vain."

"You are," she deadpanned. She bit the inside of her cheek to stop herself from smiling. "I noticed you staring at them in the line."

I gave her a "what can I say?" gesture and snickered. She rolled her eyes and bit into her half of the sandwich.

She caught me smiling down at my sandwich. "What're you thinking about?"

"Showing you all my favorite spots out here," I admitted. It was great to be home. I loved sharing memories here with my good friends.

She agreed so we walked around to all my favorite places from when I was a kid. The Daiso. I got a little red lipstick for my costume for 2 bucks. The Quickly's for some milk tea with lychee jelly. I pointed out where they used to have the Barnes and Noble store. Hollister. We each got a pair of blue jeans that I paid for. She made a joke about shoving me into the dressing room and giving me head. The Ynka store. We didn't buy anything. But we laughed at a shirt with Sitting Bull on it that said, "So… you trust the government, huh?" A cute, quaint bookstore that sold hand-me-down and new books for anywhere from half to three-quarters the retail price. We also didn't buy anything there. We walked into Bath & Body Works to smell their perfume samplers. She made a joke that if I smelled like that more often, she'd fuck me every day.

"You're terrible, girl, you know that?" I playfully nudged her with my elbow, smiling awkwardly over my shoulder as a family walked by.

"Aww," she cooed. "What would you do without me?"

I laughed forcefully as we sauntered out with her playfully

clinging onto my arm.

It grew quiet as we walked. My mind wandered to the last time I'd come here with Red and Asia. The three of us went into Hollister and gawked at the prices with boba milk tea in our hands. Then we watched Tag once we finished. Several years before that, the three of us pretended to be a throuple at the other mall in town, holding hands down the halls and everything. We ran into a friend working at Lids and she couldn't stop laughing. She joined us in the hand-holding, and we jumped in circles while she laughed about us being a polycule.

She proposed that we watch a movie so we did. There was still a bit of time until I wanted to go to the airport anyway. We took our seats as the trailers were finishing. Xiomara scooted close to me and put her head on my shoulder.

"Is this okay?" she whispered.

I nodded, nuzzling my head against hers. She put her hand palm down on the armrest between us, and I would've grabbed it if she'd had her hand palm up. I wasn't sure what to do. I just left her hand alone as we sat there.

She walked me to my car after the movie.

"Don't have too much fun in New York, whore," she teased. The wind was blowing her hair around her face.

I scoffed with faux indignation. "Who do you think I am?"

She gave me a look. A chuckle rattled out of my chest. "Dude, I'm going for Asia and Red. Not to lay pipe from borough to borough."

"Need I remind you of Balkan Man?"

I flipped her off and backed my way to the car, expressing mock disgust.

"I'll give you money," she said, a smirk growing on her face. "Fifteen bucks says you can't keep your dick in your pants for at least one day." I gave her a look like that was the easiest thing in the world. "Fifty if you can do it on more than half the days. You don't have to tell me when you have sex or with who, 'cause it's none of my business." We stared at each other with a steel resolve. "You just have to be honest at the end of the week. And if you fail, *you* owe *me* the money."

Was it strange that she was making a big deal over my sex life? Yes. Did I like getting money in any way that I could get it? Also yes.

I told her that she had herself a deal.

*****

I got back to the parking garage in 20 minutes. They waved

me through once they saw my placard on the dashboard. The shuttle was there in no time. Getting off at Terminal B, Xiomara called me.

We talked for pretty much the entire time. I even kept her on the phone through TSA. I bought some earbuds so she could be her usual self, and I wouldn't have to worry about people giving me weird looks at my gate. I grabbed some food and water because I was starving and thirsty as shit. Some wrap bites and a bottle of Smart Water were $22... which I thought was *fucking bullshit*.

Once we started boarding the plane, I told her I'd let her go. She asked me to let her know when I get to Vegas. I told her I'd try to remember. We hung up.

Thankfully, I was able to nap on the way to Vegas. The earbuds I got were good at canceling noise, so I put on my slow-songs playlist that helps me sleep and conked out. Waking up, I felt a little bleary-eyed. But de-boarding was quick since I was sitting pretty close to the nose of the plane.

I had to pee again, so I made my way to the nearest bathroom. On my way, I heard someone shout, "I HOPE THAT SON OF A BITCH FUCKING DIES!" I laughed and shook my head as I walked into the bathroom.

Xiomara called me while I was washing my hands. I let it go to voicemail. I called back once my hands were dry.

"Guessing you made it to Sin City."

"Yes, ma'am." I burped loudly. "Jesus, I'm so sorry. Excuse me."

"Pig."

"Yeah, yeah, yeah."

My terminal was spherical with slot machines in the middle. I couldn't find the gate for Chicago. When I finally found it, I saw that it was right next to the one I'd come out of.

When it was time to go, we said bye again. It was another two hours to Chicago. Xiomara called me when I updated her that I made it to MDW. We talked until it was time to board again. By then, I was a lot more tired than I expected. These seats were a little more comfortable than the last ones, despite being on an older plane like the one we took.

I fell asleep thinking about my family in California. Hoping that both my parents were taking their meds. Hoping my brother and the baby were lying in bed, and that she was actually falling asleep, not just sitting up in the nook of my brother's arm, her hand in her mouth, staring into the darkness.

October 30th, 2025, Day 1 In The City

I woke up as we made a turbulent descent into La Guardia. The plane hit the ground hard. I bounced in my seat on impact and fought the momentum as I was pulled forward as the pilot hit the brakes.

I was a little bummed that I didn't get to take a picture of the skyline as we descended like I did last time. It was raining though so I wouldn't have been able to get that picture anyway.

I turned off airplane mode as soon as I could, still waiting to be able to get up and leave. Surprisingly, I didn't have anything recent from Xiomara, which meant she was sleeping despite the insomnia she suffered from most nights. My parents texted me asking if I'm okay and if Xiomara went with me. Asia asked if I'd landed yet and that I needed to text Red to let him know that I'm coming since she's got class and several meetings on campus today.

Even though it was raining, I was somewhat elated to be off the plane. I wasn't too far from the gate that I left last time I was here. I recognized the shops and the bookstore that I'm always so tempted to go into but don't want to spend anything at. Shit would be way too fucking overpriced anyway.

After the baggage claim, I went down another floor for the bus into Manhattan. The bus wasn't as packed as it was the day I came back in April. It was a nice change.

 I got a text from Xiomara.

X: "Did you make it okay?"

Me: "Yeah, on the bus now. It's raining."

I sent her a picture of me sitting with my carry on and duffel bags in my lap smiling awkwardly.

X: "Not you doing the white man smile, bitch."

X: "Want to be a white man's whore so bad?" *eye rolling emoji*

I reacted with a middle finger emoji and closed the chat.

I texted Red that I was on the bus and he said he would buzz me in once I was outside.

R: "Hey, u have the address right? I know sometimes Asia forgets to send it out."

I wanted to jokingly ask how many people they were buzzing in and for what reasons. I knew he would think it was funny, but I was slightly weirded out about the implication… especially for a woman of color in a PWI, in a neighborhood known for its large diaspora of Black people.

Since I felt a little more refreshed, I was already mentally preparing myself for the gym. Last time I came it was the end of spring so it wasn't very warm yet, but the gym closest to where they were had no central AC so it was a fucking oven in there. You started sweating right when you walked in. It was disgusting. I hoped the one closest to them in Harlem wasn't like that. I was going to do a full body workout since I missed yesterday. MWF was legs and core. TH, TR and either Sat/Sun (depending on which day I take off) were arms, chest, and back. The thing that was gonna suck the most was how the weights were calibrated. I've never been to an *Alpha Gym* where I didn't have to adjust the weights to match the effort that I put in at my home gym. Get it together, *AG*.

We made it into Harlem after about an hour. The apartment building was only two blocks away. The only part that sucked was that it was on an incline. Nothing too killer, but I was catching my breath by the time I got to the stairs and up to the threshold. I tugged on the door and it didn't budge. I tugged again thinking maybe I was tripping, I tugged it again thinking I wasn't pulling hard enough… it finally dawned on me to try pushing it. It worked.

I texted Red and I heard the buzzing of the lock opening, another push door to get inside.

R: "Elevators are a little rickety. We're on the 6th floor, Apartment L."

I was already half way up the stairs before he said the apartment number so I just kept walking. Every time I took the stairs up, I always thought of that one clip from the Adam Sandler movie *Just Go With It*, *"'Never take the elevator and always take the stairs.'"* Funny enough, I did exactly that. Unless, of course, it was a ridiculous amount or the stairs were in some secluded corner.

I knocked and he was there, cheesing as he opened the door with his arms open wide for a hug.

"What's up, bro?" I greeted.

He squeezed me in a hug and shook me a little. "Back so soon?"

"I had to come back one last time before school started up again and before you guys moved out."

I kicked my shoes off at the door.

It was a cute spot with plain white walls and a living room twice the size of their last one. The kitchen was to the right with their living room to the left. The "dining room" was just a table right in the middle of the living room.

"Asia told you we're already starting to pack shit up, huh?" He made his way to their kitchen where water was starting to boil on their mini singular hot plate.

I nodded, setting my carry-on reusable bag on the table and my duffel onto the chair on the same side as the one I was going to sit in. "Kind of the end of an era."

"Tell me about it," he said, rubbing his face with his hands, his scratchy short beard making noise as he did. He suddenly looked very alarmed. "Oh my God! Do you want tea? Are you hungry?" He started rummaging through the fridge. "We've got some Jimmy Deans, some pizza rolls. There's also these like prepped meals that we got for free on campus. There's like Mac and cheese, salmon dishes, mashed potatoes with mixed veggies–"

We locked eyes over the fridge door. I looked at him with an amused smirk. He smiled. "I'm mama bearing, aren't I?" He'd always been that way. When we ran cross country together our junior year, just before I moved from San Jose, he used to hand out waters and LMNTs that Coach brought after we finished our runs and we were stretching.

I nodded curtly. "It's cute."

He rolled his eyes and shut the fridge. "Help yourself."

I opted for the Jimmy Dean croissants and pizza rolls.

"How was your flight?" he asked as I sat down with the food.

"They were fine." I sighed, rolling my neck around.

"You had more than one?" he went a little bug eyed, steam from the mug wafting into his face.

"I had three flights," I replied, in a pretend cheery voice. He almost spit out his tea. "One to Las Vegas, one to Chicago, and now I'm here." I did a little jazz hands.

"Ghetto, broke ass airline behavior."

I laughed and kicked him playfully under the table. I knew it wouldn't hurt him. He wasn't a linebacker or anything, but he was tall and lean with veiny ass forearms that I had to mentally force myself to not try and guess what size needles I could fit into them. Medic things.

We sat together in silence while we ate. He was doing stuff on his computer, likely for work or for fun. He would definitely be sitting there coding for fun if he didn't do it for work. If he didn't have Asia to drag his ass out and take him around the city, he'd sit there and code for hours because he wanted to. Red went to some fancy Ivy League school for computer science and engineering. Now he works virtually for a large tech company on the Bay's peninsula. He muttered to himself while he worked and made really funny faces.

I snuck a picture of him and sent it to Asia. She heart reacted to it.

A: *"My silly little bean" *smiling teary eyed emoji**

I finished my food and let Red know that I was going to the gym. I changed and started walking towards the *Alpha Gym* in Harlem. It was still sprinkling a little but it wasn't too bad.

I got a text message from Balkan Man when I was about four minutes from the gym.

B: *"Has my California baby made it safely?"*

Me: *"Yessir. When do I get to see u?"*

B: *"It's rainy so I'm staying in all day. No work.*

B: *Take Uber, only 20 minutes."*

I smiled at the screen.

Me: "I just need to go to the gym and then shower. I'll also be going out to get some green hair spray paint for my costume."

He sent me kissy faces in response after heart-reacting to my message. I also heart-reacted his message and walked inside the gym.

The gym equipment was downstairs by the looks of it near the boiler room. So great! It was going to be hot as the devil's ass crack every workout.

During the breaks between sets, I noticed that my location on *F That* was updated. I started getting messages from guys saying they wanted to link, asking if I could host, asking for my pics, and wanting to go into the gym bathrooms and fuck there. Horn dogs, the whole lot of them. *F That* had a considerable amount of women on it too. There were mostly queer people on here, which I preferred. Straight women could be kind of exhausting. A few caught my eye, but I had to let most know I wasn't looking for now and couldn't host because I was staying with Asia and Red.

I got a text from Xiomara.

X: "I see it didn't take you that long to start looking.

X: Any white people catch your attention?

X: Whore."

I chuckled out loud.

Me: "Bitch, u would only know that if u were on them too.

Me: Whore."

X: "God forbid a girl wants some dick or pussy."

Me: "I want some too, bitch!"

X: "Girl at this rate, you gonna owe ME that $50!"

Me: "Fuck off!"

She heart reacted to the message and I continued working out. I did have to adjust weight on a few but not too many.

As I left after buying a protein shake from the front desk, I got hit up by some guy who was only a few hundred feet away. He was requesting to start a chat. His pics were decent enough. Well, at least his torso was. His username was *stallion*.

S: "Hey.

S: Where u at?"

Me: "Hey man, I'm just leaving the gym, heading back to my friend's place.

Me: U nearby?"

S: "I was. I was just down there for work tho.

S: I live uptown."

Me: "How far uptown?"

S: "End of the 1."

He lived far uptown. Technically, he lived in the Bronx.

Me: "Kinda far for me right now, but if I head up anytime, I'll let u know." ;)

S: "Sounds good to me.

S: U tryna get on your knees and worship this cock for hrs while I play games or sumn."

He sent me his private album of photos. If I had ears like a dog, they'd be pointing up. I looked at his pictures. Yeah, there was no way in hell I was letting him slip away. I was going to get on my knees and worship his cock for hrs while he played games or sumn.

Me: "Yes.

Me: I'll let u know when I can."

It was hit or miss on places like *F That*, but sometimes there were absolute gems like him.

X: "Not you still on The App, diva."

Me: "Not u still in my business diva."

X: "The little light in our chat is shining. I can see you're on w/o really having to check."

Me: "Just admit that ur obsessed with me."

X: "You know what?

X: I choose peace."

Me: "As u should."

She sent the GIF of Ross from *FRIENDS* banging his two fists together.

When I got back, it was Asia who opened the door for me after I was buzzed in.

"Oh my God, hi!" she chirped. She pulled me in for a hug once I got inside. "So glad you made it!"

"Sorry I'm all sweaty," I told her uncomfortably, side stepping once she let me go.

She waved a hand in dismissal, making a face. "Have you eaten?"

"Yeah, I had pizza rolls and a breakfast croissant earlier."

She had her laptop open and it sounded like a meeting was going on. "I just have a few more meetings and I should be free by evening time. Is there anything you really wanted to do today or do you want to take it easy today like you did last time?"

I was so glad we were on the same page. "Think I'm just gonna take it easy." I ran my fingers through my hair. "I don't have any green hair spray paint yet so I do need to go out and grab that once I've showered."

She gave a few suggestions to where I could go as I started getting my clothes together.

I texted Balkan Man.

> Me: "Hey, hopping in the shower now. I'll be over in like 45 minutes. The bus takes about 30 from where I'm at."

B: "Sounds good. Can't wait!"

B: "Send photos." *kissy face emoji*

I ended up getting there a bit faster than anticipated. I guess there wasn't that great of a delay on the M bus that I was supposed to take to the UES. He buzzed me in almost immediately after the directory called him to let him know that I was there.

I guess he just got a package as well. He was already at the door in sweats and a tank top, squatting down to grab whatever came.

"There you are," he muttered, smirking down at me after he rose. His accent tickled my ears. "Please. Come in."

Walking through the door, he spanked me and squeezed hard. Goosebumps erupted from my elbows to my wrists, all the little hairs standing at attention. I meandered towards his room with him behind. I looked back at him at the door frame as he put the package on the kitchen counter with a little effort, his arms bulging slightly. The dark lighting cast a shadow over his face as he turned to me and gestured for me to move in farther.

Once we were both in the room, he gently caressed the sharp bones of my hips with both hands and leaned down to kiss my neck.

"Just as beautiful as I remember," he muttered. I pulled him close to me as we kissed, tracing his back with the tips of my fingers. He gripped my ass and pulled me closer. Our pelvises collided with great force. His hot breath on my neck made my eyes shoot open as my body trembled with chills. Embers burned in my core as he sucked on my neck gently with the tip of his teeth and lips. "Get on your knees and be a good baby for Daddy."

A need for him and his manhood coursed through me. I hunched down a little as my lips trailed from his neck, to his collarbone, and finally to his smooth and musky chest. I let out a shaky breath as I inhaled him and put both hands softly on either side of his waist. Kissing and sucking lightly on his nipples, he let out a series of quiet moans while he put his hands on my shoulders to squeeze them and lead me down farther. I planted kisses on his solid abdomen, using my fingers to taunt his flesh. He was hard and jumping inside of his boxer briefs, stretching the fabric considerably. As I caressed his happy trail with my tongue, I pulled his boxers down. It sprang up and hit me in the face. We both let out a small chuckle at that. He grabbed himself and smacked me in the face lightly with it a few times. I opened my mouth while he teased me, slapping the tip on my tongue as I looked up at him standing over me.

I grabbed it with my right hand and stroked him up and down while his legs trembled slightly. He grabbed a fistful of my hair and forced himself into my throat with a loud moan. My nerves vibrated with electricity as he held my head in place and used my throat like a fleshlight, pummeling past my uvula repeatedly. I grabbed onto his ass, pulling him into me with every thrust.

"Feels just like *pussy*," he growled, his voice breaking with a whimper. He rammed into me one last time while he gripped my hair and hammered the back of that hand with a fist. I gagged around him and felt my eyes watering. My arms were shaking with the urge to please him. He yanked my head away from him. I gasped for air and coughed a little. He kept my face in hands, looking down at me. "You like pleasing Daddy. Don't you, baby?"

I nodded at him, still on my knees and looking up. I needed every inch of him to fill me up. He brought me onto the bed, laying me on my back. He pushed my knees apart and started shoving his face into my crotch over my boxers, inhaling deeply and caressing my thighs with his long fingers. My back arched as chills shot up my spine. He tossed my underwear to the side and marveled at me with his face in between my legs. His warm breath tickled my thighs. He pressed his face against it, kissing me softly. I wanted to grab a handful of hair, but he grabbed onto my hands and pinned them at my waist. A soft moan escaped my lips as he licked me up and down.

"Mmmm," he moaned, as he took me into his mouth. He took me all the way, making my legs twitch and my body squirm. He applied light suction on my tip as he let me go to say, "You taste even better than last time."

I felt the warm embrace of his throat tightening as he bobbed his head up and down, up and down, up and down. I let out a roar of ecstasy as I felt him bring me to the point of no return. He released the grip of my hands and directed them to his hair. I balled his hair into both fists as my toes curled, my jaw locked open, and my eyes rolled to the back of my head. I held his head still and pumped into him until I was a panting, quivering mess.

He swallowed every last drop, coming back several times and squeezing me from hilt to head to make sure. When the tremors in my legs subsided, he lay on top of me, our hips still gyrating against each other.

"Such a beautiful, quivering mess," he whispered into my lips. He squeezed the sides of my neck with two fingers as we locked eyes, foreheads pressed together. "I want to be inside of you so bad."

With a light hand, he brought my legs up and pushed my ankles to my ears. I felt myself getting hard again, excited to have him buried inside me. He kissed down my legs, holding my ankles together as I squeezed the sheets. His tongue slid around my hole and my breath rattled out of me. I felt him use two fingers to open me up. I bit my lip and fought a moan, my breath quickening. Once he had protection on and slathered his dick and my hole in lube, he inserted himself slowly and I readily accepted him.

Our bodies were pressed together as he got himself all the way in. We both moaned as he started rocking his hips back and forth in a rhythmic motion. I wrapped my legs around his waist as he pinned my hands at my head, digging his nails into the webs of my fingers. His eyes glazed over as I egged him on, our breathing ragged and animalistic.

"Yeah, baby," he whimpered into my neck. "Such a tight pussy. Gonna make Daddy come." I begged him to breed me as he taunted my neck with his lips. His moans became louder and higher in pitch. His thrusts became deeper and harder. Our hot, sweating faces pressed together as he plunged into me and his body shook with climax.

Our sweaty bodies pressed together, we kissed tenderly. His body was still shaking with pleasure. His heat ravaged my senses. I pined for him.

His kisses slowed down and his eyes started closing. We laid there, cuddling and half asleep. I could feel his heart pounding against my chest as it lulled me into rest.

I didn't know how much time had passed but eventually he shook me awake, still lying on top of me.

"I love the way you taste," he whispered into my neck. He kissed me, pulling my lip with his teeth as he pulled away. He quickly kissed me again. "Always a pleasure having you."

He let me get up, but even as I dressed, I felt his hands exploring my body. We held each other close, one last time while we kept kissing each other, hands on each others' waists. We snickered into each others' mouths, admiring one another.

He finally let me go so I could put my shoes on. He spanked me and jiggled my ass around. With that, I was dismissed. Leaving, I was so light-headed. Last time was amazing but nothing like that. My legs felt weak as I opened the door to the street.

It was raining again. The wind-chill was killer. I checked my phone for GPS for the nearest Duane Reade. It was one of the stores that Asia had recommended. I was just hoping they were on this side of Manhattan too. There was one, and it was just a mile down the road.

I had a text from Asia asking if everything was okay. I lied and told her I went through all the shops nearby and everything was cleared out. Now that I was out, I'd possibly go by the Spirit Halloween store.

Xiomara started calling me.

"Hello?"

"Heeeyyy, how was Balkan Man?"

I told her everything that we did.

"Jesus!" she shouted into the phone. "Bitch, how come you never did that for me?"

"Skill issue, I guess."

"You're a fucking asshole!" she laughed. "We're going to have to try some of that."

We snickered softly in the same way.

"Anyway, are you on your way to find the green hair spray paint?"

"Yeah, I'm on my way to Duane Reade right now. Thankfully Asia and Red haven't asked too many questions."

"They don't know you whore around?"

"They'd probably think it's hilarious and I'm sure that they suspect, but no, we don't really talk about stuff like that. She used to find it funny when Red and I would draw sixty-nine on each other's homework." We laughed at that. "But that's like the most sexual conversation we've ever had. That and when someone sent out one of those spam text messages that are really dirty for the Fourth of July and Red and I were reading it and giggling like middle schoolers when we were like seventeen."

"That sounds like something you would still laugh at."

"Fair."

"You're not gonna flake or not do stuff with them just to get some ass while you're out there, right?"

"I am *not* that big of an asshole!" I scoffed.

"I dunno, diva."

"Fuck you!" I half laughed, half scoffed. Two Black women passed me and made a face. "Not you, sorry!" They walked away laughing.

"What just happened?" I told her. She cackled into the phone, wheezing and sounding like a spray bottle. "They were about to show you how they do it in Harlem."

"You're crazy for saying that," I said through choking laughs.

They ended up not having the green hair spray paint at Duane Reade. Even the two CVS's I passed on the way didn't have anything remotely similar. I mean it was the day before Halloween. I ended up running into the Spirit Halloween by coincidence. My hopes were up for like two seconds, but then I saw the line wrapping around the block and down several streets.

"Oh, you've gotta be fucking kidding me!" I exclaimed. I explained the situation to Xiomara. "It's getting dark and the rain's starting to pick up!"

"What street are you on?" she asked. I told her. "There's a Target just down the street from where you are. I'm looking at their inventory and they should have three green hair spray paint bottles in stock."

"What are you, a fucking wizard?"

"Something like that."

They had it, and I was able to make it back fairly quickly with a subway ride and a few minute walk.

Xiomara let me go just before I got inside.

"I finally found the damn thing," I told them, after Red let me in.

"It took you that long?" Asia asked, wrapping her cardigan tighter across her chest.

"None of the stores around here had it." I told her in exasperation. "Blic was empty. Michael's was empty. No CVS or Duane Reade had anything and Spirit Halloween had a goddamn line that wrapped around the block. I had to get this at the Target down the street from there."

"Spirit Halloween is kinda far…"

"Damn near forty blocks down and–"

"I'd already wandered that far down anyway." I waved a hand in dismissal.

They looked at each other and then looked at me with a simultaneous, "Hmm." Oh they knew. They let it go thankfully.

"Are you hungry by any chance?" Red asked, making his way into the kitchen. "I'm making some spaghetti."

"His spaghetti comes out amazing, by the way." Asia said, looking up from her laptop.

Red looked over his shoulder with a smile, blushing. I came over to inspect the dish. It did look pretty good. The meatballs were nice and plump and the tomato sauce smelled sweet and savory. We talked a little bit at the stove and I suggested a few things that could make it taste better. My dad used to be the chef at a high end restaurant in San Jose so I knew a thing or two about food.

I came back to the table in the living room by the pull out couch that I'd be sleeping on tonight.

"In class or a meeting?" I asked Asia. She was staring at her computer screen and looked bored out of her mind.

"Just working on my thesis," she replied with a small smile. "The program is finished the week before Christmas so I'm a little more than half way done."

"What're you getting your masters in, again?"

Her lip turned up in a smile. *"Sustainability Sciences with an emphasis in Agriculture."*

That's what it was. "What does that entail?" Her head cocked to the side with a smirk. "I mean, like… I know what those words mean individually, you know." Even Red laughed at that in the kitchen. "But like… what're you researching?"

"Ah." She took a deep breath. "We're looking at more sustainable ways for farming. Stuff like using less water, taking up less land, using *less antibiotics* in ag, et cetera."

"That's actually pretty interesting."

"Right?!" she chirped. We talked about it a little more until Red came to the table with our plates.

"Oooooooo," Asia cooed, taking out her earbud and closing her laptop. "Permission to kiss the chef?"

"Mmmm." Red leaned down and kissed her.

"No kiss for your number one guest?" I teased, twirling my fork in the spaghetti.

The two of them smirked at each other and then he leaned over the table and brought his face inches from mine. I pushed it away playfully and we all laughed.

"Didn't you two do that exact same thing in the eleventh grade?"

"Nine years later and I'm still traumatized."

"Nine years later and I'm still waiting for my kiss, God dammit!" He slammed his fist on the table and we giggled and bantered for the next few minutes.

"Did you have anything you really wanted to do this week?" Red asked.

"Other than the dinosaur exhibit at the Bronx Zoo on Sunday, not really." I told them. I loved dinosaurs. "What about you guys? Since we didn't have you with us for very long last time Red, I was hoping we'd spend more time with you doing stuff that you wanted."

He cocked his head to the side to consider it. "I mean there's that Hot Pot place in Flushing that Asia and I have been wanting to go to." They glanced at each other. "Other than that...." he stared into the distance. "Not really to be honest. How long's the dinosaur thing open?"

"Sunday's the last day and they close kind of early that day too." I'd checked a few days ago. "I think it was like four-thirty that they'd be shutting everything down."

They made a face. "That's so early."

Light bulb moment. "The Museum of the Moving Image!" I nearly shouted. Asia's face lit up. "They have that Jim Henson exhibit that I've been dying to see since the first time I ever came out here. The damn place just closes so early."

"Yeah, we can do that!" Asia said. "It's on the way to Flushing and everything."

We brainstormed some other things and then I had another idea. I looked at the Coney Island website and saw that they were holding a Halloween event tomorrow. It said there'd be face painting, food, vendors, and unlimited rides with the wrist band. It sounded fun and I'd really been wanting to go back. Plus, I still needed the white face paint since I forgot to also look for that while out. Now I could just paint my face there.

"How'd you guys feel about Coney Island? Wristbands are only eighty bucks for unlimited rides and they're supposed to be open until ten at night."

We agreed, though they were a little reluctant to let me pay that much, but I told them it was in the budget so they didn't have to worry about it. I got the deal for three bands and a lunch deal from Nathan's Hot Dogs.

"We haven't been to Coney Island, have we?" Red asked Asia.

She shook her head. "It's cute. We went last time but the park was closed so it was just the boardwalk."

"We didn't miss out on much, but it was fun," I told Red. "It's like a ghetto Santa Cruz Boardwalk."

Asia threw her head back in a laugh. "Dude, you're so right."

We talked about catching a Broadway show or two, maybe a

comedy show, and going out to shop. I pitched the Niagara Falls idea that I'd been thinking about for a while now. They said it's cute but to see the actual *waterfall* we'd have to go to the Canadian side and I didn't have my passport.

For the rest of the day, we just relaxed. Red had his meetings in the room, Asia worked on her thesis, and I read for a bit. I got bored and started browsing the *F That* events tab. One thing about NYC is that there were always down ass freaks in the area. There were a lot of orgies happening, which I really wasn't into. There were some people looking for smaller group stuff and I hit up a few of them. One guy in particular caught my attention. He had a nice body and was hosting a circle jerk for Saturday night. That wasn't entirely my speed either, but I told him I'd be down to blow him and anyone else who showed up. He accepted and we exchanged pics. He said he didn't normally go for people like me but that I was hot so he'd make an exception. I cocked my head at that and questioned if I was being fetishized or not. I decided not to overthink it too much because he was hot.

I checked the Likes tab and saw that I had a few. There was a gorgeous *Desi* couple who were also exploring the city. It was the boyfriend's profile. He was looking for a third for the both of them. We matched. I sent the first message. It didn't seem like he was online so I didn't expect a message back right away.

We were all tired by 11, but we wanted to watch a movie for the night. We settled on Vampires vs The Bronx on Netflix.

"I'm rooting for the vampires," Red joked.

In unison, Asia and I said, "Traitor."

My mom called me just before we went to sleep. She asked me how New York was and if I'd done anything exciting. I couldn't exactly tell her that I'd been dicked down by Balkan Man, but I told her that I found the green hair spray paint and that Red made us dinner. She told me that she was worried about me getting into trouble out here and how dangerous the city was because she had read some headlines on Facebook about shootings on the subway. I told her that I was fine and that she didn't have to worry so much. I told her to take her meds and she told me she already did. Dad also chimed in to confirm that she did. We said goodnight and that we loved each other and I went to sleep shortly afterwards.

October 31st, 2025, Day 2 In The City

I was up on my own by 10 am. I guessed that I was already adjusted to the time difference. Last time, it took me like 2-3 days. Red and Asia were still asleep. They usually don't wake up until like noon and weren't out of bed for another hour or two.

I got ready for the gym and headed out just before 10:30. Getting there, I spotted a hot, muscle mami (muscular woman) on the leg press machine. Her legs bulged with exertion as she pushed, barely even making a face while she did it. She was wearing a sports bra with tight leggings. She was tan, tatted, and had her ears and septum pierced. When she finally got off the machine, I had to stop myself from staring too long at her sculpted ass. We made eye contact as she came back to her machine to wipe it down with the wet paper towel. I smiled and bobbed my head at her. She blushed and smiled, giving me a scan up and down with her eyes.

Halfway through my workout, I got a notification that someone nearby liked me on *F That*. Sure enough, it showed the person was less than 100 ft away. I looked at her profile and it was the lady I was just admiring. We matched and it looked like she already sent me a message. Her screen name was *Just4Fun*.

J: "Hi, you were on the leg machine earlier, yeah?"

Me: "Yeah...

Me: I was admiring ur... legs."

J: "You wanna see them up close?"

Me: "Please.

Me: Where u staying? Are u able to have guests?"

J: "I'm staying just a few blocks down. Yeah, I can have you over. My roommates are out for the day and my kid won't be around until later tonight."

Me: "Mami?"

J: "lol"

She told me to follow her after we were done. Thankfully, it was leg and core today. I was done around the same time that she was. I gave her the ten minutes that she needed to shower. Then I realized, I probably should have showered too.

"Just do it at my place," she told me, waving a hand dismissively.

We caught a few looks as we walked out together. I smirked to myself. We started talking a bit. She was a student working on her bachelor's. Coincidentally, she did have a baby girl who's six years old. She was 32. I told her about being a paramedic for the last few years– she seemed really into that. I told her about going back to school for a post bacc so I could get a higher GPA and be mentored through the medical school application process.

She lived in a cute place in Morningside Heights. She let us in and then showed me where the bathroom was.

"Feel free to use whatever shampoo, conditioner, and body wash you want."

I showered and when I got out, I was a little disturbed by how quiet it was. The door creaked open when I got out.

"I'm in here," she called from the living room.

I walked over. She'd laid out a charcuterie board with a few different cheeses and meats. I recognized them but I just didn't know what they were called. She was coming back into the living room from what I assumed was the kitchen with two glasses and a bottle of wine. She'd changed into a knitted crop top and floral shorts. "Make yourself comfortable."

I sat down next to the arm of the sofa that was sitting behind a long coffee table in front of a large flat screen TV. She came around after pouring herself a glass and downing it right after, putting her knees at each side of my hips, essentially straddling me. I huffed a laugh. She smirked.

"You okay?" I snickered.

"Just helps me to loosen up is all," she reassured me, setting the glass down and then turning her attention to me. She put her hands on my shoulders. "Working out just leaves me a little tight, you know?"

"Mmm." She leaned in and we kissed. Her lips tasted like a red blend. I suddenly grew self-conscious and pulled away slightly. "I'm so sorry if my shirt still smells like sweat. I usually–"

She kissed me to shut me up. Her fingers trailed to the hem at the bottom of it. My lips trailed her jawline as she took it off me. "Didn't think that was going to be on for very long anyway."

Her fingers explored my body as we kissed tenderly, tracing along my tight core and chest. All the little hairs on me stood at attention as a cooling sensation flooded my body. I tugged her bottom lip softly with my teeth. A little moan escaped her lips as I traced her back towards the clip of her bra and pinched it off of her.

I stared at her breasts, biting my lip slightly as I cupped them. "Fuck," I sighed. My fingers teased her nipples. I watched them perk up as our hips continued to grind together.

Our bodies were flaming coals as we held each other. She had both hands on the back of my head, holding me close and whimpering softly as my lips made their way from hers to her chest. I kissed her breasts, my fingers pressed lightly at the edges of her wide hips.

I could feel her getting wet through her shorts, dampening my own with how aroused she was. I re-positioned her with one fell swoop, resting her in a sitting position and reclined against the couch cushion. She let out a little snicker as she leaned back, arching up her hips as I made my way down from her chest to her belly with my lips. She pulled her spanks down, revealing her pink panties. I looked up at her with a smirk and she rolled her eyes. With her hands in my hair, she pulled me closer as I kissed her thighs. Her legs trembled a little.

I craved every part of her. I felt myself throb in my shorts as I shoved my face into her crotch. I inhaled her scent and rubbed my face around her. A whimper escaped her lips. Her fingers tightened their grip in my hair. My fingers traced their way slowly up her thighs to her hips. I slowly pulled her panties down, moaning with my face in between her legs.

Primal instinct took over once her panties were around her

ankles. I pulled her closer to the edge of the couch so that I could have full access to her. Her legs tightened around my head and she gasped for air and her entire body tightened as I focused on her clit. My tongue circled gently around her hood. She played with her breasts and moaned as she moved her hips around to the pace of my tongue laps. Her fingers ran through my hair and pulled me closer as her body shook, she gently muttered, "*Fuck*, papi."

I introduced one finger into her, causing her breath to rattle out of her. I kept savoring her taste, moving the one finger in and out slowly with a beckoning motion. After pulling my shorts off with the other hand, I stroked myself slowly. My desire for her made me ache for a release. A moan rattled through me as she squeezed my head again with her muscular thighs while I edged myself to the brink. I inserted another finger and felt the ridges and grooves of her tightening walls. While licking her up and down and pulling away with slight suction, I whimpered into her as she quivered underneath me with a growl. Riding the last wave, she locked her ankles around my neck and didn't let me go.

Her legs continued to shake around my head, as I rested buried in between her legs. She egged me on and snickered slightly as I grunted into her, my whole body trembling. I panted in between her legs, still kissing her softly.

She ran her fingers through the front of my hair and pulled me away from her, looking down at me. She huffed a laugh and pulled me up to kiss me.

After a few minutes, I pulled away slightly. "Sorry for making a mess on your floor," I told her, still on my knees. My cum lay in a massive pool right in front of me.

We laughed. She told me where the towels were. I went to get them naked. She watched me clean it up with an amused smirk, now sitting on the edge of the couch.

"Put that down," she ordered.

I let it go. She pulled me in to kiss me. She kissed down my neck and took a deep breath. "You are far too pretty to be out on the streets like this." We locked eyes. "How long are you out here for?"

"Just the week," I let her know. "I've been out here twice before and it never feels like long enough."

"Mmm." She wrapped her arms around the back of my neck as we made out for a few more minutes. She then pulled herself away. She smirked and got shy. "I swear I don't normally do stuff like this… especially not with younger people."

"Mmmmm." I mimicked. We snickered softly and kept kissing. "I'm glad I got to be of service to you, *princesa.*"

She raised an eyebrow and bucked her head back. *"Tú habla' e'pañol?"*

"Claro que sí, mamacita." She slugged me playfully. *"¿Eres dominicana?"*

We bantered back and forth for a bit in Spanish then kept making out, periodically feeding each other cheese and meat and sipping the wine on the table.

"Do I get to see you again?" she asked, pulling away after a longer kiss. She seemed embarrassed to ask.

"Maayyybbeeee." I kissed her again. "Isn't your kid's presence going to complicate things a little?"

"Only for the weekend. She's at school pretty much all day for the week." She grabbed her curly hair and put it up into a bun. "You said you're leaving Wednesday?"

"Yes ma'am."

She smirked and rolled her eyes. "Don't be a stranger." She kissed my forehead, then leaned away. She exhaled sharply. "Gotta start cleaning up before my kid gets here."

I huffed a laugh. I got up and put my clothes on (they did smell like sweat). She walked me to the door. I kissed her goodbye. "You are so fucking hot."

She giggled and blushed. "I'm Teresa."

"Cameron."

"Do your friends call you Cam?"

I chuckled, looking slightly down at her. "They do."

"See you later, Cam." She kissed me. We were both cheesing as I left the apartment and headed back to Asia and Red's.

*****

Red was up and in the dining room when he opened the door for me.

"Is Asia still asleep?" I asked him softly.

He nodded and put his finger to his lips. I gave him a thumbs up as I took my shoes off at the door. He gestured to the stove with his pen. There was breakfast made. It was *huevos rancheros* with a little bit of rice and refried beans.

Red started speaking softly into his mic while clacking away at his keyboard as I sat down to eat. He said bye after a few minutes of me eating. "Figured you'd have worked up an appetite." He smirked. There was a hint of playfulness there in his eyes. I wasn't sure if he knew I'd hooked up with someone or if he was just giving me shit because he knew it was something I would do.

I huffed a small laugh. "You have no idea."

"Feel free to finish it." He closed his laptop. "I don't think Asia is going to want any when she gets up." He sounded slightly annoyed at that.

Once I was done, I did rinse off again, finally able to actually change. When I got out, Asia was up and at the table looking a little grumpy.

"Good morning sunshine," I teased.

She exaggerated a smile. "Good morning!" She opened her laptop. "Was there anything you wanted to do this afternoon? Red has some work to get done before we get going. If so, I do need to work on my thesis for at least a little bit, but I'll be good so don't feel bad. I did also want to get going at least by like three-thirty, four-ish that way we get to Coney Island before dark."

"Nah, I didn't really want to do anything," I told her, leaning back in the chair. Then I shot forward in my seat. "What're you and Red going to dress up as?"

"Oh, I'm just gonna be Kim Possible again."

"Is Red gonna be Ron?" I joked.

"No, but that is such a good idea!" She laughed.

He did end up being Ron, just the ginger version and not a twink. He put on a baggy black top and some cargo pants. Asia had a black jacket with camouflage bottoms and a crop top. She did her make-up lightly, but she looked stunning. She helped me with the lipstick and the smudging. She put dark circles under my eyes and the three of us had optics on my hair as I used the hair spray paint. My hair was so dark that it wasn't really showing up, but it did once we were out and in the waning, natural light. I wore Red's black Timberlands. They fit pretty well, only a half-size bigger than mine.

On our way to the subway, we got a few compliments as people walked by. Trick-or-treating was already starting. I looked at the clock on my phone. It was already 5. We were a little behind schedule, but I didn't think it was too bad. We walked the 10 minutes to the D train to take it all the way down to Coney Island.

When we got to the train platform underground, someone started calling for me. "Excuse me, Mr. Joker, Sir!" They were obviously drunk. Half their face was covered in fake blood.

"What's up?" I called back, walking backward so I could still pace to where we were going but face them.

"Can I get a picture with you?" they slurred. Their friends immediately started protesting and apologizing to me, telling me that I didn't have to. *"Están chingando y ya dijo* he's cool with it, *foo."*

She wrapped her arm around me once I reached her. She smelled like tequila, lime, and cotton candy. Red and Asia sat there laughing as her friends took reluctant photos of the two of us.

"I don't know if you're a man, woman, or whatever, but you

sexy Mr. Joker Sir."

Her friends pulled her away and kept apologizing, telling me that I was a rock star for entertaining her.

I gave them a thumbs up and laughed as the three of us kept walking to our side of the platform. While we sat on our Brooklyn-bound train, my mind started wandering as it usually does when I'm commuting for a long period of time. The compliments and the fiasco with that lady sort of went to my head. I knew I looked good. Having people tell me though sort of unleashes another can of worms. I daydreamed a bit. Not about that girl, but about Joker's baby girl, Harley Quinn. It'd have been hot if I ran into her at some post-Coney Island Halloween party and danced with her, feeling her up either on the dance floor or in some secluded corner. I would have loved to make her mine. It made me all hot and bothered just thinking about it. The packed D train certainly didn't help. I ended up having to take off the blazer, just wearing the white button up and green tie with HAHA!s in black ink all over it.

Our car was almost empty by the time we reached the Coney Island stop. The sun was making its final descent on the horizon. It probably would've been really pretty if there weren't so many goddamn buildings in the way. It was pretty chilly outside so I was able to put the blazer back on.

"God, I fucking hate the wind," Red moaned, putting his hands in his pits.

"Big burly man friend bested by the wind." I joked.

We laughed. Approaching the block just before Coney Island, the lighting from the streets hit just right. The wind blew powerfully and it bit alright, but Asia's hair danced magically. She was stunning one hundred percent of the time, but right now, her beauty was scintillating in the dimming light.

Getting closer, we could see that it was somewhat of a ghost town. "It'd be so fucked up if they closed early." I looked around. There was hardly anyone here. There were workers, but there were maybe only a handful of other groups present.

We ate first. Asia and Red were so relieved to be out of the windchill. Eating messed up my lipstick a little bit so Asia helped me reapply it.

"Something tells me we're not going to be able to get my face painted white tonight," I joked. She huffed a sad laugh. "It's okaaayyy." I assured her. "We still have time to have fun."

Once we ate, we got our wristbands and started getting in line for rides. Looking around, there were even less people in this segment of the park. There was one worker on stilts as some kind of creepy scarecrow/jester/clown, waving their torches around at people as they passed. Even that worker looked bored out of their mind. We got on the swings first.

I guess I looked bummed out on the swing as we waited for it to swing because a parent of one of the kids that was a few seats in front of me shouted, "C'MON JOKER, SMILE! THAT'S YOUR WHOLE SHTICK!"

Asia, Red and I started laughing just as the ride started and we began our ascent and forward movement. Getting off, Asia showed me some of the pictures she took. I was right–I did look good. There was one just before take off that's a side photo of me staring straight ahead and kicking my feet. I did look and wave at her a few times, but I didn't know she was taking pictures. Those ones were pretty cute too.

We were only able to get on two more rides. Even though they said it was going to close at 10, they started closing up at 8. I got kind of pissed but didn't want to make a scene in front of Asia and Red. While we were in line to get on the Ferris wheel, we saw someone dressed as Batman that was about to get off. When we saw each other, we stared each other down and I did the "I'm watching you" gesture. Him and his buddies got a good kick out of it. We rode the Ferris wheel and it went up pretty high. We got amazing views of the darkened beach, the park below, and the Cyclone Coaster across the street. I snapped a few pics of the two on my phone. It was cute how much they actually looked like Ron and Kim Possible.

"Cuutttiiiiieeesss," I said, showing them and then sending them the pictures.

Next, we rode the ride that we'd heard people screaming on when we first arrived. It was little planes that rotated at extreme angles and then eventually went upside down as they soared back to the ground and then back up again. It made my asshole clench quite a bit. Just when I thought it was going to be over, it sped up again. I groaned in protest. It was fun though, but also a little terrifying.

We got pictures in the middle of the grounds where it looked a little like a pumpkin patch. Someone offered to take pictures for us. I was ready for them to stop, but then they insisted we start taking silly ones. I looked to Asia and Red and they were already squatting and getting into spy poses. It felt weird doing it as the Joker, but it was really funny nonetheless.

"You guys are so awesome!" she shouted, giving us our phones back. "Have a good night, y'all! Happy Halloween!"

I felt kind of shitty leaving. I was so excited for this night and even though it felt a little fun, I felt bad for hyping this up and bringing us all this way just for the fucking park to be closing. Now I felt even worse about them wanting to repay me for the bracelets. I didn't want them to have to pay for something that ended up kind of a bust.

As we were exiting, Asia pulled something up from the park's official Instagram page. "Apparently, they announced they'd be closing on their social media?"

"Fucking Coney Island," I scoffed genuinely upset.

"YEAH!" Red shouted from behind me, making me jump in fright. "FUCK YOU, CONEY ISLAND!"

"FUCK YOU, CONEY ISLAND!" Asia joined in.

I looked back at them and they were grinning from ear to ear and silently laughing. I threw my head back and cupped my hands over my mouth. "FUCKING CONEY ISLAND!" They kept laughing, falling over themselves. "CLOSING EARLY AND SHIT!"

We were catching a lot of stray glances as we stumbled down the street clutching our sides.

Once we settled down, we made it back to our train.

One of the things we talked about doing earlier was watching the movie *Bugonia*. "Hey, I guess we can actually watch that movie tonight." We caught the showtime in Union Square for the nine forty-something. We'd make it with a few minutes to spare after we got whatever it was that they needed from a convenience store nearby.

Bugonia was… such a clusterfuck of a movie in the best way possible. It was a little slow in the very beginning, but then it picks up quickly after they kidnap the CEO played by Emma Stone (not a spoiler, it's in the synopsis). I love the expressions that Asia and Red make so when the plot twist of the movie hit, I looked to my left and caught them staring at each other then at me.

Though the night didn't go as expected, this was pretty nice. I couldn't really figure out why I still felt like something was missing.

We got back to the apartment within the hour. We could hear that there was a party going on a few doors down.

"Sounds like they're having the time of their life," I commented, taking my shoes off at the door.

"Oh yeah, they throw fuckin' ragers," Red laughed, pulling his baggy sweater over his head.

Asia was taking off her jacket when there was a knock on the door. I moved out of the way so that Red could answer it.

It was one of their neighbors. He was dressed as Patchy The Pirate from SpongeBob. "Hey! I just wanted to come over and invite you guys to slide through!"

The three of us looked at each other kind of awkwardly. "I mean… we kinda just got back home…" Red trailed, looking to Asia and I to help him out.

"But you guys are still wearing your costumes," he insisted, pointing at Asia and me.

The three of us raised our eyebrows and cocked our heads to the side. "You know what, you're right," Red agreed, throwing his baggy sweater back on. "Let's go?"

We followed him out. The apartment was only a little bit bigger than Asia and Red's, but there were about 80 people packed in here. Over in the kitchen area, about 15 people were playing rage cage on the table. To the far left was a really big balcony with a lot of people dancing on it. The living room was packed with people dancing, drinking, and standing around in groups talking really loudly.

Walking through, I had to do a double take on this one chick. She was really dressed like Harley Quinn from *The Suicide Squad*. It didn't look like she had her Joker either. She was standing in a group of other lady villains, DC and Marvel. I felt Red pull me a little towards the balcony as one of her friends pointed towards me. The girl spotted me and smiled, walking over to me.

Red and Asia noticed and gave me a knowing glance and a smile.

"Hey you," she greeted. "I've been looking for you."

"You look good," I complimented her, having to shout over the music.

"You should dance with me." She held out her hand. I hesitated because I felt bad. I was supposed to be here with Asia and Red, not dancing with some random chick that I didn't know. "Oh, come on. You don't wanna dance with your baby girl?"

I looked at them, feeling bad but wanting it so badly. It was just a stupid dance but ever since the subway ride, I couldn't get it out of my head.

"When in New York, bro."

I took her hand and then twirled her around on one finger. Her friends cheered and assured her it was fine for her to leave them hanging. We went with Asia and Red to the balcony where there were a few other couples dancing around. It wasn't very big, but it was oddly roomy enough for everyone there to dance together in their own little space. Occasionally, there'd be an elbow brush or an accidental step on someone's heel, but no one took offense.

We danced pressed together, her face in my chest and her arms wrapped around my neck. My hands were around her waist and my face rested on the top of her head. Even though we were only six stories up, the view was still quite breathtaking. I absolutely loved the way cities looked at night, especially this one.

"I feel like you owe me a little bit of information about yourself," she said, looking up at me as we kicked it up a little and waltzed to the music. It was a little toned down since the glass door filtered out a lot of the noise from inside.

"There's nothing about Daddy you don't already know, baby girl."

She scoffed a laugh and rolled her eyes. "Shut up."

I let up with a small huff laugh. "My real name is Cameron. I'm a paramedic in California. I'm on the precipice of becoming a student again so I can get into a good medical school. I live in a small one bedroom apartment down the street from both of my aging, disabled parents. We have a dog. *They* have a cat." She giggled with glee as I booped her nose with one finger at each pet. "And I'm here with those awesome people over there." I nodded towards Asia and Red. Asia was now sitting on the balcony ledge with her legs wrapped around Red's waist and his arms wrapped around her torso as they made out. "They're a little strange but they're big softies and I love 'em to death."

"That's so sweet," she chirped. Her eyes twinkled in the dim light. "I'm Sarah. I'm a nurse here in Manhattan. I'm *fucking done* with school." We snickered, pressing our foreheads together. "I just adopted my younger sister from our... unfortunate parents. We don't have any pets..." I winced playfully. "yet! And those were my ride or dies in there. They're really cool people, but I'm glad we're out here because those girls would've eaten you alive, poor thing." We both threw our heads back and laughed at that.

She pulled me closer for warmth as a vehement gust of wind ravaged the balcony. "Is life treating you well lately Cameron?"

Not the hard-hitting questions, I thought. "You know... everything is finally going my way for once..." I trailed. She huffed a small laugh and we locked eyes. "But I can't help but feel like something is wrong... like I don't deserve any of this."

She gave me a sad smile and caressed my cheek with a soft hand. "You deserve everything from the moon and back Daddy."

I snickered into the top of her head. "Thanks baby girl."

I looked at Asia and Red, still eating each other's faces. "At least one pair out here is getting some." I scoffed at her. She giggled as she looked up at me. I leaned down. We kissed. "Let's go back inside?"

I looked back to my friends. "I'd feel bad leav–"

"I don't think they're going to notice," she giggled. She had a point so I let her guide me inside, looking over my shoulder a few times. I felt a tad guilty, but she was right. I didn't think they were going to notice either.

We went inside and walked to the back of the apartment. The first door she pushed on opened quickly and the room was empty. She pushed me onto bed. We made out for a long time. I started fingering her until she was whimpering as she kissed my neck. She begged me to let her show Daddy what a good girl she was. I was getting ready to take the suit off but she stopped me. I guess she thought it was sexy. She unzipped my pants and moaned once my underwear were fully off and she shoved her face into my crotch. God, she really was such a good girl. I leaned back on one elbow, my other hand holding her head down and running my fingers through her hair. I told her what a good girl she was as my legs started shaking and I wrapped my legs around her neck.

When I came, she cleaned up every last bit of my mess. I collapsed on my back, panting. She laid on me with the pants still around my knees. We made out for a while, our hips grinding together as she moaned, whispering sweet nothings into my lips.

In the next second, I needed her off me. I needed us to stop doing this. I needed to go back to my friends because I was here for them and here I was being a disgusting whore. They were probably searching the balcony, looking through the living room and kitchen, worried sick that I'd wandered off and gotten kidnapped or something.

I sat up abruptly.

"What's wrong?" she wondered, alarm in her voice.

"I have to go." I told her, leaning forward and jumping to pull up my pants. "I'm not being a very good friend right now and–" My hands were shaking as I buttoned the pants. I could hear my heart pounding in my chest. The room almost felt like it was about to start teetering. "I just have to go. I'm so sorry!"

I don't really remember how or where I found them. I just remember them being really worried, grabbing my hands as I profusely apologized for leaving them alone on the balcony in the cold. I remember sitting in the chair shivering as they brought me blankets and offered to help me change. I guess I blacked out because the next thing I remember is being in the bed with the apartment entirely dark and the party still raging a few doors down.

I sat up and ran my hand through my hair. Deep down, I knew what was happening, but I wasn't ready to admit it. I didn't allow myself to think that I let myself get this bad.

I was slipping again, and I didn't know if I was going to be able to stop myself...

November 1st, 2025, Day 3 In The City

I woke up feeling fine but with a bit of head fog. I remembered everything–well mostly everything. I still wasn't sure how I found Asia and Red or how they found me. I didn't remember changing, but I remembered the events that led up to all that. I remembered feeling like the walls were going to close in on me and that I couldn't breathe. That poor girl, I really hoped she didn't think I didn't like her.

I could hear the shuffling of footsteps in the hallway. It was Red. When he saw me, he blew out a long breath in relief. He sat on the edge of the pullout and wrapped his arms around me in a bear hug.

"Dude," he scoffed. "Are you okay?"

I nodded with my head in his chest. "Yeah, I'm okay. I just have some head fog right now. That's all."

He recounted finding me wandering the apartment like a lost puppy, muttering their names under my breath with my hands clasped over my ears. Once I realized who they were and that they were trying to take me out, I kept insisting on going to check on Sarah. I was hell bent on making sure she was okay. They eventually got me to let up. That's when I started shaking uncontrollably and crying. They got me out of the costume and put on the pajamas I was wearing. He said I laid there hyperventilating until I finally passed out.

"You don't remember any of that?" he asked me. He'd already let me go and we sat side by side, facing each other.

"Only bits and pieces," I told him, rubbing my eyes.

"Was that like…" he swallowed. "Was that like a panic attack or something?" I nodded, getting the sudden urge to cry. He gave me a sad look and pulled me back in for a hug. "Is there anything else I can do to help you?"

Just him saying that made me weep like a baby. He squeezed me and rubbed my back as I cried into his chest. I didn't know how to express my gratitude so I just sat there with him until I pulled away when I could hear Asia stirring in bed and then shortly after shuffling in the hallway.

Red cleared his throat and blinked rapidly. He went into the kitchen as Asia peeked her head out from the hall.

"Morning," I greeted, my voice still laced with emotion.

"Hey," she said sadly, coming to sit by me and rubbing my knee. "Are you feeling okay?" I nodded. "We don't have to go to Flushing–"

"We're going to Queens," I interrupted. I was not going to ruin their plan to go to Flushing and get Hot Pot. "I will go to the Museum of The Moving Image if it fucking kills me." The three of us laughed as I wiped my face and then my nose on my sleeve. "I'm okay. Do I still have time to go to the gym? I just have to do that and then shower if that's okay."

"Oh yeah," she assured me, standing and pulling her chair out at the table. "It's still pretty early. We weren't going to leave until like ten-thirty."

I checked my phone. It was only 8:12 am. Damn, I was never up this early on a day off. I brushed my teeth and then headed out. It was a little bit cloudy, but the weather report on my phone said that it was going to clear up pretty soon.

I got to the gym in 12 minutes. No Muscle Mami in sight this time. Well there were, but none of them were Teresa. I gave myself a mental pat on the back for bagging a MILF as I got on the bicep curl machine. Not my first time with a mom and not the oldest woman that I'd slept with, but it had been a while.

Xiomara called while I was in the middle of my set.

"Hey girlie," I answered.

"Heeeyyyy," she responded. "How's everything going?"

I wasn't going to tell her about my panic attack last night. I knew that she was someone that I could go to when I was going through it, but I had my friends here. "Doing alright. I'm just at the gym right now."

"Okay gym rat, look at you."

We talked for the duration of my workout and as I walked back to the apartment. There was a Halal guy at the corner across the street from Capitol One Bank so I stopped and got a chicken gyro for breakfast.

"What're you getting at the halal cart?" Xiomara asked me after I told her to hold on so I could order.

"Just a chicken *gyro*," I told her.

"A what?"

"The *gyro*," I said again.

"Bitch, I'mma need you to speak like a white girl for a second."

I cleared my throat and did my best Valley girl voice. "A chicken jye-roh."

"Not you being that bitch that says Ih-beeth-a and bar-theh-lona," she laughed. "Fucking headass."

"Girl, shut up," I laughed. The Halal guy gave me a look and I shook my head, waving my hand at him.

After getting my food, Xiomara started telling me about her plans for the day and the *Dia de los Muertos* event that they had on campus this weekend. She was helping set one of them up. They were selling *cempaxochitl* at a lot of boutiques and floral shops in town. Xiomara was raving about how so much of it was inauthentic and that so many people were raising the prices and making it almost inaccessible for the people who actually celebrated it.

I'd forgotten that it was *Dia de los Muertos* to begin with. I felt kind of bad that I wasn't at home. We celebrated every year. Not with the *cempaxochitl* or anything, but we lit candles and had our little *ofrendas* for my great-grandmother, my dad's aunt and uncle, and our cousin Mari who'd passed away two years after we moved to Merced. We kept our old dog and rabbit's urns with their ashes inside of them nearby too. When I have the money to do so, I would love to have a whole shelf/wall of an *ofrenda* for all of them. I was hit with a pang of emotion as I started thinking about the memories with my loved ones from when I was a little kid. How lucky I felt that I got to meet them and be loved by them, and how my love for them persisted long after they left this Earth.

We said bye to each other as I got to the apartment building and I wiped my eyes before ringing either Red or Asia on the directory downstairs. They looked just about ready to go by the time I got up there, which made me feel a little bad that they were waiting on me. I tried to hurry up in the shower for their sake.

Once I got out, they looked just about ready to go so we left. It was gorgeous outside and it was nice to see them wearing clothes like they were going out and not in costumes or something for school. Red was wearing a black trench coat over khakis and the Timberland's that I wore last night. The sunlight made his hair glow. Asia was standing a little away from him closer to me as we chit chatted about whatever the fuck. She had on a light grey sweater quarter zip and baby blue jeans that hugged her legs nicely with Uggs dupes. I felt like I stuck out like a sore thumb next to them. I just had on a blue zip up from my alma mater with washed blue jeans and the ratty ass sneakers that I brought with me. I pulled my phone out when they weren't looking and took a picture of the both of them. Asia caught me so she was looking my way with a half smile and a hand in motion giving the peace sign while Red was staring off into the distance, deep in thought about something. The curved street and city infrastructure was in the background.

Asia came up to me to see. "Oh my God, that's so cute," she said. "I love how you can see the motion of my hand." She examined it a little more. "Looks like such a quintessential New Yorker photo." She kept contemplating it. "The background is gorgeous." She looked up at me, her mouth stuck in a smile. "You have a really good eye for pictures."

"Aww shucks."

Red peered over. "What're y'all talking about?" I showed him. He snickered. "Nice!" He did a double take. "Damn, I look good." We teased him about being vain.

We took the M106 into Queens heading towards La Guardia. The bus was packed as shit and because they were getting ready for the marathon tomorrow, there were a couple of detours in Manhattan. A lot of the passengers started getting angry and one of them made a comment about feeling like they were being kidnapped by their bus driver. Of course, kidnapping isn't funny but someone who's barely making a living in the most expensive city in the country definitely isn't doing it with the CCTV watching.

Asia and Red looked really cute sitting together. He had his arm wrapped around with her face nestled into that little divet between his pec and his armpit. She had one hand rubbing his left thigh as they watched whatever it was that was playing on his phone, sharing earbuds.

Due to the horrendous traffic, it took a while to get into Queens but once we got in, we transferred to a Q bus to get us closer to the museum.

We were supposed to take a train up to the museum from where we got off, but with the subway delay, it was faster to just walk so that's what we did. We walked through a cute neighborhood in Astoria. Once we got to the building, there was a long ass line that we thought was to get into the museum. Thankfully, Red asked to make sure it was for the museum and it wasn't. It was the voting line because the museum was also a voting site.

We were all able to get student tickets even with my raggedy ass student ID from my alma mater. Asia offered to pay even though I'd allocated money for any museums in my trip budget, but she insisted so I just let it go. Whatever saved me money, I wasn't going to gripe about too much. Plus, it'd be money I could use for my courses once school was in session.

Even though we were instructed to start on the 3rd floor, we didn't really like listening and ended up taking the exhibits one floor at a time, starting with the first floor. There was a large screen showing some kind of anime with really cool graphics. But I wasn't that interested, so I trekked up to the second floor. Asia and Red followed, confused and laughing a little bit that I was gone and had left them behind.

The second floor is where they had the Jim Henson exhibit with the Muppets, *Sesame Street, Fraggle Rock* and more. There was a large wall with different clips from the shows, movies, and interviews done with the characters over the years. It made me a little emotional looking at it. When I was a kid, my parents used to put on *Sesame Street* to calm me down. We would do the counting and the singing. Then, when Luke was born, we did the exact same thing. I remember having so much fun with him growing up. I missed him so much.

There was a really cute little section where you could record yourself playing with the puppets and make a little movie. I just about lost it when I saw a mom and her kid playing together, laughing and having a good time. I missed playing with my dad like that and I wished that my mother had been more present to play with me and Luke like that. I had to step in a lot as Luke got older because Mom and Dad had to keep working longer and more frequent hours as bills kept accumulating. All the things that they missed out on. All the things I had to sub in for–

I had to step away before Asia and Red noticed me crying. I pulled myself together in a corner by a life-sized Big Bird behind glass. I rubbed my face and looked into my phone camera to make sure my eyes weren't too puffy. They weren't, but it did look like I was crying.

Walking into another section, I found Asia and Red wandering around separately, looking at different cameras, rolls of film, and books of still frames on display. Luke and Dad would love this place.

Before I knew it, I was on the phone with my brother.

"Hello?" he answered in a sleepy voice.

I forgot it was still before 11 am on the West Coast. "Hey…"

"You good bruh?"

"Yeah!" I replied, huffing a laugh and then sniffing. "I just wanted to call and tell you that I miss you."

"Oh…"

"I'm at the Museum of The Moving Image right now with Asia and Red." I felt both pairs of eyes flash my way at their names. "They have a really cute dedication to Jim Henson and it shows the Muppets and *Sesame Street* and all that…"

"That's cool. We used to love the Muppets." He did his impersonation of Pepe The King Prawn talking into the fan in *Muppets From Space*. "Build it… and they will cooooommmm-meeee okaaaayyy."

We snickered into the phone. "You know I was thinking–"

"Uh oh." We laughed again softly. "You are thinking a little too much out there, huh?"

I smirked. "Probably. But uh… I was thinking that uh… maybe next time I come out here, I can bring you with me."

"Yeah, I'd like that." His voice cracked. He cleared his throat. "I think that'd be fun."

"We can bring the baby…" My eyes pooled with tears. "And I dunno maybe Mom…"

"Yeah… I know Dad's not taking his ass on an airplane so he's out for that."

We both laughed. "I was just thinking about going to Albuquerque a few years back. I miss traveling with you."

"Yeah, we had a lot of fun that week."

"I loved it because when we were little, I always wanted to just take you away from everything going on at home." So many glimpses of our childhood flashed in my mind. "Run away, you know? Start our life somewhere new." We snickered. "No but… I do want to bring you here eventually."

"Mkay," he yawned. "Just let me know."

We talked a little bit longer about the baby and what they had planned for the day.

"I'll talk to you later though. I love you and I miss you too."

"I love you too."

I didn't realize that I was full-on crying until I saw a tear splash on an exhibit plaque. I felt Asia and Red standing on either side of me, not really saying anything but giving me both the space and the company that I needed.

Red put his arm around me and squeezed my left shoulder. Asia nuzzled up against me and wrapped her arms around my waist as I put my arm over her shoulders. Nobody said anything. We just sat there holding each other until I was ready to start walking around again.

They had a cool Ancient Egyptian pyramid themed theater room that was playing an old 1950s episode of Superman. I thought about my grandmother telling me stories about her watching these kinds of cartoons with her siblings and dad when she was little. I remember telling her she had a cool dad. She told me she was glad that I had a cool dad too.

The final floor was dedicated to *Mission Impossible* movies. I didn't realize there were that many. I wasn't really a fan of Tom Cruise anyway so I wasn't very enamored or even impressed with the exhibits. Some of the stunts were cool, but that's about it. The most memorable thing was Asia saying one of the side actors had an "ugly ass mustache" in one of the last movies. That made me laugh. She doesn't curse very often which is why when she does, it's hilarious.

Asia was hoping that there'd be some movies playing since they normally have select showtimes for indie films by underground directors and actors. I guess today just wasn't one of those days. Nonetheless, the three of us had enjoyed ourselves so we started heading out and made our way to Flushing.

Asia and Red started raving about these egg custard treats that were sold at a local Chinese pastry shop. We ended up getting some after we went into a Chase so they could pull out some money.

I always forgot that Red's dad is half Chinese. I was reminded every time he'd speak Mandarin or Cantonese with a perfect accent.

"*Xièxiè*," he thanked them.

He ordered 6 of them in total so that we'd each have two. There was a little table in a corner with two chairs that I was eyeballing. The Chinese lady sitting at the table next to it alone with four chairs saw us coming and offered a chair, turning it around and pushing it towards the table so we could all sit together.

"*Xièxiè*," I thanked her. Terribly.

She grinned widely with a small giggle and replied in perfect English, "You're welcome."

The four of us shared a laugh and then we ate our pastries.

"These are called *pastel de natas* in Portuguese," I told them. That's why they looked familiar. I'd had them before a while back when I dated one of my old Portuguese friends from elementary school.

They offered to buy the actual Portuguese ones because they did sell them here, but I told them I'd tried them plenty of times and that this was enough.

Red smirked. "Say that again?"

"Pastel de natas?"

"I love it when you talk dirty," Red groaned with his mouth full, gripping a napkin and biting his lip.

"Red!" Asia japed, smacking his shoulder. "Not in public."

I was silently wheezing and holding my sides. It was so unexpected yet so Red. He was normally good about his setting when being inappropriate.

They started talking about this salon that came up on their social media feed on the bus ride into Flushing that apparently did really good haircuts. They'd been wanting to get something different for awhile and since I was no longer in need of slightly longer hair for my costume, I agreed to getting one with them. It fit perfectly too because it was still a little too early for the Hot Pot Dinner.

It was just a few blocks down from where we were and just two doors down from the Hot Pot place. It wasn't super busy so the three of us got sat down pretty fast. They washed Red's and my hair first since ours were shorter. Asia got hers washed, but then had to sit with her hair wrapped in a towel like a beehive until hers fully dried.

"How much off?" the stylist asked me. She had a thick Vietnamese accent.

"I can show you," I told her, pulling up a picture from July.

"Show me!" she said, a little too excited to see the photo. "Your hair is so pretty." She ran her fingers through it and started with small snips with the little scissors.

"Do you have a boyfriend or girlfriend?"

I laughed. I mean shit, people have told me I have bisexual vibes, but I wasn't expecting to be clocked by my good Viet sister in Queens.

"No."

"Too bad," she pouted. "You are so gorgeous."

Asia and Red were giggling on either side of me in their chairs. Red's hair was starting to look pretty different. Asia's hair was still wrapped up. She chatted with my stylist for a bit in Vietnamese. At one point, Asia said something and the stylist repeated it with bug eyes and gripped my shoulder.

I raised my eyebrow at Asia in the mirror.

"Eleven years of friendship!" the stylist squeaked. Her eyes narrowed to slits as she smiled. "You like family, huh?"

My chest warmed. I couldn't help but smile sheepishly. "Has it really been that long?"

"Yeah, we met in twenty fourteen," Red chimed in, swiping at his freshly coiffed hair in the mirror. He already had a bit of a blasted fade but now it was just fresh, more defined, and a bit shorter. They shaved him too so that he no longer had his short beard.

That was the worst year of my life, I thought. The year my anxiety and depression started to rear their ugly heads. The year that Mom and Dad almost got a divorce and Dad had to live out of motels for a while. It was the year I really struggled with my sexuality. When I tried opening up about it to my parents, I was dismissed and told I was just going through a phase. The year that my grades started to kind of slip. I was passively living my life. I didn't want to die, but I just didn't see the point of living. "Damn," I huffed in a small laugh. "It doesn't even feel that long."

I looked at myself in the mirror as she continued to cut my hair. The circles under my eyes looked darker. While I felt fit, I looked weak in the mirror. My arms looked nothing like Red's. My chest looked flat and not shaped like it used to be. My stomach was flabby and not solid anymore–

"Do you like it more curly or more straight?" she asked me.

"We can keep it a little curly," I told her. She started working my hair with some type of pomade and curled the hair closer to my forehead in a middle part and rounding at the sides. It was like a somewhat curly haired version of a praying mantis/money piece hairdo that I thought was so cute on other people. I tried doing it myself most days, but it usually didn't work out because of how naturally wavy my hair is. It could kind of work because my work-hat usually helped flatten it out.

"Okay stud," Asia complimented. She was finally getting her hair tended to.

Red and I had to wait a bit for them to be done with her hair and in total, our cuts were only about $80. I think hers was more expensive since her hair was longer. Asia's hair cut was extremely cute. They made it a little more round to shape her face. She looked so adorable.

"Fucking snack," Red murmured as we walked out. Once we got out, he grabbed her face and kissed her.

"Behave," she warned, pulling away and snickering.

"You behave," he quipped.

My stomach growled. "Do we have reservations or…"

They laughed. "Yeah, I got them this morning," Red told me, slipping his arm around Asia's waist as we walked out and towards the restaurant.

For looking like a little hole-in-the-wall place, it was actually really big on the inside. The waiting area was filled with a couple of other parties waiting on their time slots. A few were dressed in business formal attire. I won't lie, they got me a little hot and bothered.

The hostess came up to us to ask about our seating arrangements and Red started talking to her in rapid Mandarin. She looked very taken aback but also very delighted. Her reaction pretty much sums it up the first time anyone hears him speak the language.

After a few minutes, the hostess led us through a common sitting area. I thought we were going to be sitting out there, but she kept taking us farther. It was a room with several other people that had lanterns all around the room that shimmered and glowed. There were Chinese pillars laced with gold and a sparkling chandelier in the very middle.

"Oh my god, this is gorgeous!" I exclaimed, walking in circles with my head glued to the ceiling. "How'd we luck out with this?"

Red chuckled softly and got a little… well, red. "This is for you, buddy."

I whipped my head towards him, feeling bad that he must have spent so much money on this. "Red, you shouldn't have."

"Why not?" Asia objected as we started sitting down at the circular table with candles in the middle of it. "We have so much to celebrate."

I thought about how amazing it would have been if a bottle of champagne just appeared out of nowhere as he started rattling off the things we had to celebrate and we toasted to it.

"Yeah," Red agreed like it was obvious. "Eleven years of friendship," he nudged my foot with his under the table, "you getting into your post bacc program," he grinned comically and shook the table a little bit, "and somebody's birthday is coming uuuuuppppp."

I chuckled at his animation. "Red, your birthday is before mine."

"Yeah exactly," he started, "I wouldn't do all this shit just for you."

The three of us laughed as our server came to let us know how the hot pot was going to work. Everyone at the table had to get the same deal. It was two soups with the standard additives that the most basic meals came with and then there were multiple upgrades that included things like seafood platters and other types of more expensive add-ons that I didn't really pay attention to. I was already hyperfixating on the seafood platter because it looked fucking bomb. It was to come with crab legs, oysters, salmon, and a few other things. We got the most basic one that came with the seafood platter.

Once we had drinks, we did a toast: to our friendship, to getting into the program, and to Red and I's birthdays coming up. His birthday is on the 22nd and mine is on the 24th.

Red stayed attentive pretty much the entire time. He served us our food after the thinly sliced wagyu slices would cook to perfection. I think my favorite parts of the soups were the broths. The tomato was my favorite. The seafood platter was absolutely stunning–especially the fish filets. Within the hour, the three of us ended up getting really fucking full.

The waitress insisted that we take these little personal tubs of Haagen Dazs ice creams. I knew that it was going to make me shit so I only took a few bites with the little wooden spoon that it came with. While we were savoring the ice cream and making small talk, Red got a phone call from his dad.

After answering in English, I could hear him getting his ear chewed out and watched him pull the phone away from his ear and make a face. He started speaking to him in Mandarin while shaking his head. I snickered a little at his reaction and Asia smiled.

"He's been really hard on Red lately," Asia commented, scooping some of her ice cream into her mouth. "Something's going on with their family right now, I guess."

"Damn," I sighed, looking to where he'd just exited the room.

Red came back looking very distressed. His eyes were red. He sat down next to Asia and couldn't make eye contact with either of us.

"Red, what's wrong?" Asia asked, her eyes wide with fear and worry.

"So…" his voice broke. He swallowed the lump in his throat. He covered the bottom half of his face with one hand and grabbed Asia's hand with the other. He started shaking. My heart sank at how hurt he looked. What the fuck happened? "Um–" his voice cracked. He closed his eyes and silent tears started streaming down his face. "Everything's fine with my dad. It's just, umm…they just made a bunch of lay offs at work."

"Oh my fucking God?!" I spat, dropping my chopsticks into the bowl of my food. Asia was expressing similar horror.

"Streamlining most of the jobs with AI, I guess," he growled.

Asia and I rolled our eyes in disgust. "What the hell do they expect you to do now?"

Red let out a long huff of breath. "I was just talking to some coworkers. We're gonna brainstorm and write each other letters of rec." He rolled his eyes and whoop-de-doo'd with one hand. "I'll be flying out Monday or Tuesday depending." He balled his fists onto his eyes and took a few deep breaths.

I had no idea what to do to help besides be there. I didn't want to reach my hand over the hot ass stove so I kind of just sat there until they both indicated that we were going to start heading out. The plan had been to get boba tea in a shop nearby but we ended up getting a Q bus to the M106. We didn't say much as we commuted back, but we both held onto Red or did our best to stay as close as possible.

A movie had been on my mind, the Bruce Springsteen movie that my dad really wanted to see was out. Even though I'm not a Bruce Springsteen fan, I was a fan of Jeremy Allen White. I thought he was cute in *Shameless* when it was still running but that definitely wasn't going to happen now. A different movie could be what we needed at least as a distraction for the night, but I wasn't going to say anything until they asked if there was anything that I wanted to do.

Once we got back, Red went to the room so that he could make some phone calls. Even though the walls were thin, I couldn't really hear what they were talking about. We were able to tell when he was done because the entire apartment went quiet. After 20 minutes, he still wasn't out. Asia pointed to the room and mouthed that she was going to go check on him. I gave her a thumbs up and a nod of understanding. After 20 minutes, they weren't out. After another 40, they still weren't out. I lost track of time by the time they did come out, their feet dragging down the hall.

Red's newly coiffed hair was slightly messy. His eyes were puffy and his cheeks were tear-streaked. I got up to hug him and he trembled in my embrace. We sat down and I dragged my chair from that side so I could sit next to him.

He sighed deeply and wiped his face with one hand before he started explaining what was going on. "Don't worry, we're not gonna end up homeless or anything," he croaked. That was somewhat of a relief. His face fell again. "I just really liked my job, you know?" He swallowed.

It looked like Red tried to jump start his joy, not wanting to wallow anymore. "Tell me about your job, dude. What's the difference between an EMT and a paramedic? You're a medic right?"

I huffed, a little annoyed because it felt like he wasn't letting himself feel his flurry of emotions, but I usually try to change the subject too, especially once I feel like it's no longer of use. "They're both emergency medical technicians. EMTs are trained in basic life support. Paramedics are trained in advanced life support. Paramedics can start IVs, give drugs that EMTs can't, do advanced airways–like intubations–and cardiac monitoring. We run the codes and command scenes during mass critical incidents."

Red sniffed and wiped away the last of his tears. "Hell yeah dude." He was able to compose himself and kissed Asia, telling her how much he loved her. Then, he smirked and looked at me. He playfully kissed my forehead quickly and I shoved him away, wiping it with playful disgust.

Red made plans to catch a flight out on Tuesday since it was the earliest that he could get out. He was going to switch it to Monday though, if he could. He packed quickly and organized a few things that he could take with him to San Jose and leave there for when they do move out.

After that, we agreed to watch a movie together. At first, we really couldn't decide on what and had half a mind to rewatch Vampires vs The Bronx, but Asia had the good idea to watch a movie on HBO Max that'd come out earlier in the year. Red and I agreed because it was with that lady from Fifty Shades, Captain America, and the hunky dude from The Mandalorian… and the protagonist really fucking pissed me off. Spoilers ahead, her character–whatever the fuck her name was–was not supposed to get back with her ex. Yeah he has a nice ass or whatever, but their communications skills were fucked, if they ever even actually fucking existed. She refuses to do any type of introspection on how she views herself or her relationships with other people and probably doesn't even fucking see herself as worthy enough to get with a man who's going to do the work of having good emotional intelligence, but I digress. Asia and Red pretty much agreed, though Red was being a little bit of a rage baiter.

"I don't even really see the perks of marriage," Red started. Asia side-eyed him and bit her inner cheek, daring him to keep talking. "I mean other than like tax benefits."

"Sir!" She warned.

I laughed silently as Asia continued to stare Red down as he broke down into giggles and continued to shrink until he was hugging his knees and laughing into his legs at the corner of the table.

"I love you boo bear," he wheezed, looking like a tomato and holding a stitch in his side.

"You can sleep out here with Cameron tonight," she quipped, standing up and tucking in her chair.

"At least now I have a chance of being a little spoon!" he called to her as she went down the hallway.

November 2nd, 2025, Day 4 In The City

We didn't cuddle. Asia called him to bed shortly after that, though I likely wouldn't have been opposed to it.

Looking at my phone, I got a Google Calendar reminder for my Zoom meeting with my advisor tomorrow. Thank God I had that reminder. I would have completely forgotten.

Today was my day off so I wouldn't be going to the gym. I did however still want to go to the Bronx Zoo. I would feel kinda bad going without them, especially since Red had seemed interested in going to see the dinosaur exhibit, but it was already 11 and I couldn't hear them stirring in the room at all. In fact, I'm pretty sure Red was snoring but then other than that, there didn't seem like there was going to be a whole lot on the docket today. So it probably wasn't going to be that big of a deal? I wrestled with myself–feeling especially bad because I also didn't want Red to feel like I didn't care about him when he needed friends now more than ever, but ohmygodohmygodohmygodohmygod. He did have Asia. I was going to go to the goddamn dinosaur exhibit and ride that fucking monorail. It was the last day of the season and I didn't know when I would be in the city again to do something like this.

With my newfound resolve, I ate super fast, showered, and changed. I was out before noon and it was only about a 40 minute train ride up.

Walking to the 2 a few blocks up, I noticed that I had a few messages on *F That*. It was just that guy saying that he was sorry about having to cancel the circle jerk that was supposed to have happened last night. I told him not to worry about it because I totally forgot about it anyway. The other message that caught my eye was the guy who lived super uptown checking in on me and asking when I was available to go and see him. I let him know that I could potentially do it after I went to the zoo and he agreed. I'm not gonna lie, thinking about him aroused me a bit. Walking through the turnstile, I had to shake my head a bit and run my fingers through my hair. I needed to focus on getting to my stop, not get distracted with dick on the brain.

The Bronx Zoo was only a few blocks away from the stop off of 178th St. It was a cute little walk. I guess they offered reduced prices for students, but when I asked the lady at the booth she said it was for New York students only. *Bullshit*, I thought.

Walking through and heading towards the Asian monorail, Xiomara called me. We chatted for a bit and I turned on the video call for her so that she could see the animals as we rode along. The monorail was a cute little train with a view of a bunch of different cute animals that you could see in Asia. They were mostly hooved like deer, goats, antelopes, bison, etc, but there was one really cute elephant and male tiger there too. The conductor talked about whatever it was that he was talking about and also played short pre-recorded audios about the animals that were present and the different types of efforts that the zoo was a part of to help with the conservation of wildlife.

"Are you making your way to the dinosaur exhibit now?" she

asked as I made my way over. I told her that I was. "Ugh, I wish I were there with you to see it. I really wanted to be a paleontologist when I was a kid. I was obsessed."

"Oh my god, that's so cute," I giggled. "I didn't necessarily want to be a paleontologist, but I did have these Leap Frog flash cards that had hundreds of dinosaurs on them. It had their names, pictures of them, their diets, and whether they were Triassic, Jurassic, or Cretaceous dinosaurs. I used to carry them around everywhere and I used to write little stories about dinosaurs going to school and shit."

"Aww, Cam!" she cooed. "That is like the cutest thing you have ever said."

Once I got to the dinosaur exhibit, I turned the camera back on. Xiomara was in awe the entire time, gasping and pointing at the screen like she was actually there with me. Her reactions were really cute. It was a trail that had ginormous animatronic dinosaurs on the outer parts of the trail with a mesh wire fence to keep people off the exhibits.

Strangely enough, I wasn't oo-ing and ahh-ing the way Xiomara was. This was one of the things that I had been looking forward to the most but for some reason, it felt like just an ordinary day, like I was just taking a stroll as a part of my everyday routine.

"That was so cute!" she said after she saw that I'd finished walking through.

"It was huh?" I replied dryly.

I walked around, still talking to Xiomara. It wasn't until we were off the phone that I realized that I was lost. After asking someone where the main gift shop was, I found my way. I passed by a couple small exhibits and saw a lot of peacocks on the way through. There were families with their kids and babies, taking pictures of each other and of the animals. I could imagine having the baby with me, holding her in my arms as I trekked down the paths while she pointed at the different animals with big eyes and mouth agape. I would read the plaques to her and tell her the names of the animals in both English and Spanish and maybe once she was able to walk, Luke and I could chase her down the stone walkways while she went after the rogue peacocks or went to pet people's dogs that they brought with them. I saw a sign for their Night of Lights event coming up. It was a few days before my birthday. If we ever lived here, it'd be the perfect opportunity to see it with the baby and Luke–hopefully Mom and Dad, too.

I found the main gift shop and walked inside. I got matching mugs for Asia, Red, and me. They were white mugs that had a lion with the words Bronx Zoo on them. I texted Xiomara to ask if she wanted anything. She said anything would do, so I bought her a mug with animals in rainbow stenciling.

My stomach growled as I walked out, not even feeling hungry before that, but I decided I should probably eat. I got a personal pizza and some fries. Setting my stuff down and starting to eat, I became exhausted. I didn't even feel like I did that much work today. Yes there was the walking, but I walked everywhere all the time. Not only that, but I lost my appetite about halfway through eating. It wasn't a lot and it tasted just fine. I didn't want to give it too much thought because I didn't want to sit there and ruminate/catastrophize and self-diagnose with an eating disorder or slow onset hypomania that made me not as hungry. I kept eating and tried not to think too much about it because I knew that I was going to need the energy.

My phone dinged and I saw that *stallion* from earlier was hitting me up to check on me.

S: *"Hey bro, u still gonna come thru?"*

Me: *"I'm leaving Bronx Zoo rn. Addy?"*

He sent me his address. He told me it was easier to take the Bx9 bus to the nearest 1 station and take it all the way down, so that's what I did.

He buzzed me in once I got there. I felt on edge for some reason, despite having done this a million times before. I was eager to get on my knees and service him for quite some time. I day dreamed about that hot body and gorgeous dick as I walked up the stairs.

He was waiting for me at the door, leaning against the doorframe, shirtless. His pictures must have been a little outdated because his abdomen didn't have as much definition as it did in the pictures he'd sent me, but he did look the same for the most part. His sideburns had grown out a bit and he was rocking a handlebar mustache like Pornstache from *Orange Is The New Black.*

"Come on in," he greeted, opening the door wider and stepping inside. It was a studio that smelled like mothballs. There was a twin sized mattress in a corner by a sliding door that led to a balcony of some sort. The only light that was on was the light above the stove. It didn't illuminate anything besides two pans that looked kinda dirty from here. There was an entertainment center with a large flat screen and a PS5 tucked underneath it. "Make yourself comfortable. There's water in the fridge if you want any."

After getting the water out of the fridge with literally nothing besides the water in it, I went over to the bed, plopping down quite far. I put the cup of water on the wooden chair that was next to the bed.

He laced his fingers through mine on my left hand and pulled me closer. He wrapped his arms around me and we kissed for a bit. His mustache was prickly. He looked at me hungrily after he slipped my shirt off. Then, he traced my nipples with his calloused fingers and kissed my neck. I ran my fingers through the back of his hair as he did it, kissing the top of his forehead. I moaned softly as he tugged on them gently with his teeth. My body felt like it was vibrating as he ran his fingers lightly through my leg hair.

After another few minutes of making out and feeling each other up, he huffed a small laugh. In the very dim lighting, I could see the hint of a smirk. "Can I be totally honest with you?"

I rolled my eyes and snickered softly at him. "I'm used to men only lying to me so some honesty would be quite nice."

He ran an affectionate thumb across my cheek with his fingers under my chin as he gazed at me. "You're funny." He kissed my forehead and looked at me, biting his lip. He sighed. "To tell you the truth…" he sighed, looking sheepish, "…I've been yanking my shit for hours." That was hot. "Thinking about you coming here to service me made me *so* fucking horny, I couldn't help myself."

"So what's the issue?" I pondered.

He laughed, his head lolling back a little. He rubbed his right shoulder with the opposite hand. "I'mma nut hella fast, I just know it."

"Okay," I shrugged. I reached for the waistband of his shorts. "I didn't come here for nothing." We both laughed in shock and I profusely apologized for sounding like such a guy with a one track mind. "I'm so sorry. I didn't mean it like that."

Through his giggling, he muttered, "Nah, you good. You're hella funny."

He held my face in his hands as our lips collided again with my hand in his shorts, stroking him from shaft to tip.

My hand was covered in his pre-cum by the time he took his shorts off. My mouth was watering when he ordered me onto my knees. I listened, eager to serve him even if it was just for a minute or two. When he stood up, his cock swung like a chandelier, fully hard but sagging from the sheer weight of it. I caressed his shaft in one hand, his balls in the other. I licked him slowly from shaft to tip, tip to shaft, and shaft to tip again. My fingers cradled his balls softly making him gasp. He blew a lengthy breath through his lips. He moaned as his knees started shaking.

"Damn baby. I'm gonna come," he whimpered. His body quaked as he rammed into me, holding my face in his hands. I gagged violently against him, tracing my fingers on the backs of his legs while he used me like a rag doll. He cried out and almost lost his balance as he twitched in my throat, emptying every last drop.

I wasn't done with him yet. Even after he slumped back onto the bed, I laid on my stomach and kept nursing on his softening penis, playing with his balls and kissing the tip every time that it came out of my mouth. When he couldn't take it anymore and was practically begging me to stop, he yanked my hair and pulled me off his dick, shot into a seated position, grabbed my face, and kissed me more fiercely than he had since we started. He laughed a little.

"That's enough, you greedy cum slut," he growled and kissed me again. We took turns tugging on each other's lips with our teeth.

We made out for a while longer. After a bit, he started kissing me less fervently and loosened his grip on my ass while I straddled him and held his face in my hands.

"You okay?" I asked, pulling away and looking down at him in a sitting position.

"Yeah," he whispered. His throat bobbed as he swallowed. "I'm just getting kind of tired, not gonna lie."

We made out a little more, both of us on our sides facing each other, my arm wrapped around his back. He gave me one long kiss on the forehead before his kisses stopped altogether and his grip on my hand in between us went limp.

*****

I walked out of there a nervous wreck and shaking. I noticed my lock screen had several notifications from Asia and Red.

A: *"Hey! I don't know if you went to the Bronx Zoo, but if you did I hope you had a wonderful time!"*

A: *"Are you doing alright? I know the zoo is almost closed."*

A: *"Hey, we're grabbing lunch nearby. Did you want anything?"*

R: *"U ok?"*

R: *"We're going to an Ethiopian place down the street tn, u joining us?"*

R: *"The sun is starting to set Cam. U good?"*

As I walked to Broadway and W 242nd, I could hear my heart pounding in my ears. *I'm a bad friend*, I thought. *I'm a bad bad friend.* My vision was tunneling and the ground started to undulate. I nearly collapsed onto a nearby trashcan and puked all over it. My body trembled as I dry heaved and spat. I got several stares and one person asked if I was okay. I waved them away as I started unsteadily towards the subway station entrance. I was hyperventilating when I got to the turnstiles and had to lean against the wall to steady myself.

Five. Five turnstiles with back and forth traffic.

Four. Four wheels on the cars that are driving by- honking, screeching, blinking.

Three. Three cracks on the wall that I'm leaning against.

Two. Two puddles of piss in the corner with a strong odor.

One. One small tear in the side of my tongue, releasing the taste of iron into my mouth. Blood.

I spit the blood out of my mouth, standing up straight and closing my eyes as I took several breaths in through my nose and out through my mouth. A security guard approached me and asked if I needed medical attention. I shook my head no and put my earbuds in, tapped my phone against the reader and walked through the turnstile.

*****

I got into the apartment after Red buzzed me in and opened the door. "There you are," he teased. He took on a serious look after getting a good look at me. "Hey, what's wrong?"

I scrunched my face to try and make it look normal and shook my head. "Nothing really," I sighed, kicking my shoes off. My hand started shaking the second I took it off the wall, I couldn't lie now. "My anxiety's just kinda been kicking my ass all afternoon."

I hobbled over and their faces turned down in frowns. "Are you okay?"

"Yeah," I lied, shaking my head to snap myself out of it. "Is it okay if I make myself some tea?"

I stood up abruptly and almost fell. They both stood up, ready to help me. I huffed a small sinister laugh, feeling like my body was betraying me. The three of us made tea together.

"I have some ashwagandha root in the cabinet here," Red told us, reaching into the overhead cabinet with ease and grabbing a jar of it. "This shit works wonders."

We had some tea together and it was probably just a placebo effect, but I felt instant relief from my anxiety once I swallowed my first sip and felt it warm my throat, chest, and belly.

"How was the zoo?" Asia asked me, setting her cup down and using the hot mug to warm her hands.

"It was nice," I told them, a smile tugging on my lips. "The animals you get to see on the monorail are so cute." I showed them some of the pictures I got to take.

"Oh my god, those are the cutest things!" she gushed.

I told them about the dinosaur exhibit and getting lost. I showed them the matching mugs that I got us, which they also gushed over and walked around the table to hug me for. I told them about seeing the Night of Lights poster. They told me they'd heard amazing things about it but never got the opportunity to go or had anyone to go with. We talked about how much fun it would be to go together, how I thought about maybe one day taking Luke, the baby, and our mom out there. While making a joke about my family living and working out here, I noticed a subtle change in Red's expression. I didn't want to bring it up, but after a few minutes he did bring it up himself.

"I was able to move the flight up," he told us, sighing and looking up at the ceiling. He threw a hand up in defeat and let it hit the table. "They're literally just fucking giving up on us, you know?" Asia had her arm wrapped around his waist and I held his hand over the table, trying to be as reassuring as I could.

Getting himself out of it, Red asked if we were ready to go out to eat at that Ethiopian place. We both agreed. Asia grabbed his face and kissed him, brushing his face with her thumb affectionately the same way that *stallion* did to me in his studio.

We walked a few blocks down to the Ethiopian place for food. It was a cute little place with African decorations meticulously placed around. There was a seating area near the windows on the right when you walked in with little wooden chairs and a bean bag chair. We got seated at a little table on the other side of that, in good view of the flat screen that was set just over their bar.

The menu was fully online so we had to scan a barcode that was on this little cube. I hadn't been to an Ethiopian place since I was like 7 years old so I had no idea what to order or what any of this food looked like. I felt like an idiot and I didn't want to ask what the dishes were because the ingredients were written in their descriptions. I settled for an appetizer of chicken sambusas. Asia and Red got chicken and beef tepsi. I had no idea how that was going to look, but the servings were huge. The bread was almost like an unrolled crepe and the meat itself was so good.

Red covered his mouth with his fist as he chewed and asked, "What's your post bacc gonna be like?"

"It's fully online this upcoming quarter, thank God," I told him, taking a bite of the sambusa after. "And we also don't have the in person seminars until the beginning of April for spring."

"What're the seminars for?" he asked, resting his face on his fist as he leaned forward.

"It's to prepare us for the med school application process. It's to help us secure shadowing opportunities, interning, and stuff like that."

He and Asia asked more clarifying questions, leaning in and getting giddy for me as they ate. I got a little bashful talking about it. It was really sweet that they took interest in what I did. They asked if I had advisors or anything like that and I told them that I did and that I had a meeting with mine tomorrow at 9:30 PST.

We ate all of our food and headed back to the apartment afterward. They wanted to play a game of Monopoly Scrabble. It's basically Scrabble but when you score, you move your Monopoly pieces and how much you move correlates to the points you got from the words. It ends once the bag is empty of letters and the first person uses all of theirs. The winner is the one who has the most money once the game is over. Red won.

While they were putting it away, one of my friends from TikTok who lives in Brooklyn messaged me on Instagram.

H: "Hey! I'm in Harlem right now! Would you be free by any chance? I'd love to grab a tea or coffee with you before going back to BK."

I said yes. Last time I was here, I'd wanted to hang out with her and she told me she was too sick to do so but we agreed to see each other for sure next time. Since she's a lawyer by day, I knew that she was pretty busy.

"Hey, one of my friends in town wants to grab something to drink. Did y'all wanna do anything else tonight?"

They shook their heads and I started getting ready. I was on 122nd Street and she wanted to meet on 144th Street. The buses were going to take forever so I made the trek from Adam Clayton Powell Jr. to Broadway and then walked up the 22 blocks that went by pretty quickly.

She was sitting at a table under a heating lamp outside. When she saw me, she jumped up in excitement.

"Cameron, hi!" she cheered. She threw her arms around me in a bear hug. Her long black hair tickled my ear. "Oh my God, it's about time we got to meet face to face."

We caught up about what's been going on in our lives. She was engaged and I was still single. They moved into a new apartment together. My parents lost their home of ten years and had to live in a small apartment. Her parents were thriving and doing well. My parents' health was deteriorating. I told her about the heart attack and how Mom was forced into retirement after breaking her hip at work. The arthritis was getting worse and was affecting how much they could walk without a cane or walker. She was a licensed professional, and I was getting ready to go back to school to eventually become a licensed professional. Another one, anyway.

"How're you feeling about the possibility of having to leave the state? You know... if you get into a med school out here or somewhere where the winters would be miserable for them if they wanted to be closer to you?…"

"Well, I've talked about it with Luke," I sighed. "He said he was willing to take the reins of some stuff while I'm away."

"What if he can't do that? What if he has more kids or moves himself, you know?"

A part of me was a little pissed off that she was so worried about it, but she had a good point. I sighed deeply, letting out a long breath. "We'll figure something out, I guess."

"I know you will," she smiled. "You're you."

I smiled, feeling a little sad.

"What's wrong?" She reached her hand over the table.

"I just…" I sighed, getting a little emotional. I swallowed the lump in my throat. "If I do have to move away and Luke isn't very available… I'm scared that there isn't much that my parents have to live for. I don't think they've got like a suicide pact or anything. I just…" my voice broke, "…I don't think they know how to live for themselves, you know? My whole life they've done nothing but be my parents. I'm just afraid they don't know how to not be. I don't-" I blinked and a tear fell down my face. She squeezed my hand reassuringly. "I don't think they see any value in their own lives outside of Luke and me." I sniffed and huffed a laugh. "Sorry, I've done nothing but cry on this damn vacation."

She gave me a sad smile. "You're too good for this world Cameron." I made a face. She snickered at me. "You've got so much love to give to everyone around you, more than you know what to do with."

I'd never thought about it that way. I didn't want to keep crying so I just shrugged. "I guess so."

We finished our tea and she gave me a big hug before she left. "Now the next time I see you in New York City…" she gave me a stern look, "… I better see a white coat stitched at the *chichi* with Cameron Mancía M.D!" She did a gangster voice with the credentials for emphasis.

We laughed and squeezed each other's hands in reassurance. She waved goodbye.

I was back at the apartment around 9:30/10 pm.

"Hey, you made it just in time," Red greeted, his eyes twinkling.

I made a face. "In time for what?"

They both grabbed a hand each and dragged me into their room. I had half the mind to crack a joke about us finally bringing the polycule to fruition but decided against it.

Red threw the door open. "Ta-da!"

My jaw dropped, fell off of its hinges, hit the floor, and plunged its way through the Earth's crust. They used the time that I was gone to make an *ofrenda* of my family members that have died over the years. They had their family members on there too, but the largest center piece of it had the pictures of my loved ones. It was decked out in *cempaxochitl*, dollar store candles, and necklaces around praying hands.

"You guys…" I muttered, covering my mouth with my hand. I huffed a small laugh as my eyes welled with tears. "All I do is fucking cry on this vacation."

They snickered sadly and hugged me from either side. Asia spoke softly with her cheek on my shoulder. "We knew how much it would mean to you. I know it's your first *Dia de los Muertos* away from home so we wanted to bring it here for you."

I tilted my head back and breathed deeply a few times to prevent the tears from falling. *Oh my god, I loved my friends* and they loved me, too.

Asia started talking about her aunt that was on there. She laughed through tears as she reminisced about her babysitting and how they used to have so much fun together when she was a kid. She let us light some incense for her and showed us how to bow and place it on her mantle after saying a Buddhist prayer in Vietnamese. Red told us about his grandparents who'd died in middle school. He didn't remember too much about them, but they'd both remembered who he was in their final moments as they beckoned him to their sides on the hospital beds. I told them about my cousin Mari and how she used to crack me *UP* whenever we'd hang out. I was so lucky to have ever been able to meet them.

After standing there for a few more minutes, I started laughing uncontrollably. Red and Asia looked horrified at first, but then started laughing through their own silent tears.

"We are so fucking sick and twisted," Red half laughed, half sobbed, rubbing at one eye with his palm. Asia agreed, nodding as she kept laughing and crying while trying to dry her eyes with her sleeve.

My friend Harmonia's words rang in my ears, *You've got so much love to give to everyone around you, more than you know what to do with.* I think that's the reason that I started laughing. This was our way of showing our loved ones that we love them. That despite them having left this world, they live on through us. Their existence persists through the love that we feel for them, despite it not having anywhere to go.

That night I dreamt of my funeral, who would go, what they'd say, and if my wishes would be honored. I was there, sitting in the front row. I always thought it'd be cool to have a pre-funeral before we had the real one. For my closest friends and family members to be able to see me normally one last time. That is, of course, if I was dying from something terminal like cancer. It hurts me to think of my parents being there. I didn't want them to have to endure that. Hell, I don't even really want my brother to be at my funeral. I want him to die first, only because I know I could handle it. I've known a world without him. He's never known a world without me, but in this dream, they were all there. Young and barely starting to grey, barely able to make it through their eulogies because even though I was sitting right in front of them–alive– they knew that someday much sooner than they'd ever hoped, I wasn't going to be. That's what hurt them the most about whatever pain they'd ever have to endure.

I woke up crying pretty heavily. I lay there with my face buried in my pillow, unable to get any relief from the pit of despair that was growing in my chest. When I couldn't cry tears anymore, I rolled onto my back and stared at the dark ceiling.

A siren wailed in the distance. And I felt more empty than I'd felt in a very long time.

November 3rd, 2025, Day 5 In The City

"Hey, buddy. We overslept. We're leaving in five minutes." Asia and Red were hovering over me while he shook my shoulder.

"Guys!" I scoffed, face palming and kicking the blankets off me. I rushed into the bathroom to brush my hair and teeth quickly so that we could go. At one point, all three of us were in there occupying the same space, nitpicking at our hair and fixing our quick outfits.

I grabbed a big ass box that weighed like 40 pounds. Asia had a heavy bag on each shoulder. Red had a duffel bag slung around one shoulder and wheeled two suitcases. Fuck a taxi, fuck a $90 Uber ride. We lugged this shit all the way to the 125th Street A train station and took that bitch all the way down to Howard Beach at JFK. Did we get stared at? Yes. Were people checking out my arms as I held 40 pounds and walked up and down platforms and stairs with it? Also yes. It was a nice little ego boost.

Red checked in all of his bags with the airline once we made it up from the train platform and the Howard Beach shuttle. The box I was carrying was the only issue, it had to be wrapped so I had to carry it across the damn bag drop and have some dude wrap it up on a machine that reminded me of a cotton candy maker.

We walked with Red right up to the beginning of TSA pre-check. He kissed Asia the way that she kissed him last night. Since my arms were free, I wrapped my arms around him in a bear hug as he leaned over. For not showering, he smelled really good.

"Bye," he said, letting a suitcase go and wrapping one arm around me. "Thank you so much for coming this week. I can't wait to see you again. I love you Cam." He kissed Asia over my shoulder. "And I love you more."

"Love you too," we said in unison.

The two of us backed away so we could watch him walk away. "I'm so jealous of his ass," I confessed. She threw her head back in a laugh and a few people stared. "Straight men with fat asses are such a waste of potential." She shoved me playfully while rolling her eyes as we walked back to the Howard Beach shuttle station downstairs.

We got back on the A train after paying the fee for using the Howard Beach shuttle. "Are we getting off at 125 again?" I still had my advisor meeting at 12:30 and I could've sworn she'd said she had a meeting at the same time, if not within the hour.

"Yeah, we can do that," she said. She had a light bulb moment. "Oh! Did you want to see a Broadway play today? I've been trying to get lottery or rush tickets all week. I guess it's just a busy season or whatever."

"Oh yeah! Yeah, I'd be down for that. What's on Broadway right now?"

"I know Hell's Kitchen is out right now. It's Alicia Keys' story."

"Oh, dude. I fucking love Alicia Keys!"

We found which theater it was showing at online. The plan was to go up to the box office and ask for rush tickets. They'd be even cheaper because Asia was a student at Columbia.

Once we got off at Times Square, I noticed that I had a lot of notifications. It was mainly my parents trying to make sure I was okay. My dad sent me a few pictures of the *ofrendas* at home with lit candles.

Dad: "Lit candles for Nana, Mari, and our babies."

I huffed a small, sad laugh. I loved that he simplified it to lighting candles. He knew the significance of course, but he can't spell in Spanish very well. Oh papa. My mom was checking up and sending pictures of her and Dad getting food around Merced. Luke was sending pics of the baby.

I had a couple more likes and matches on *F That*. I checked my DMs and Muscle Mami from Halloween messaged me this morning.

MM: "Hey Papi, I didn't see you at the gym this am."

Me: "Hey princesa! I was in a bit of a rush to get my boy to JFK.

Me: We overslept and everything."

MM: "Sounds like a busy morning lol

MM: My girl's going to be at school the rest of the day if you got any time to spare.

MM: I know you got your friends and stuff tho."

I told her that I'd see what I could do. Another message from the same app came in.

MFCouple: "Hey hottie, my lady and I are looking."

MFCouple: "It looked like u were closer earlier."

Me: "Hey! I'm in Times Square right now, but I am staying in

Harlem off of 122nd.'"

MFCouple: "Dope! We're free pretty much all day. When are u gonna be free?"

Me: "I've got an advisor meeting at 12:30 that should only last about an hour."

MFCouple: "Sounds good. Keep us updated."

We found the theater pretty quickly. We went in and asked for student rush tickets and they were thankfully available. Fuck paying full price. I covered the tickets since it was only $78 for both.

By the time we got back to our station on Broadway, it was 12. "Hey, what time does it say we're going to make it back?"

"It's an almost forty minute ride back up." She cringed a little.

"Fuck," I cursed. "Let me just email my advisor real quick. Let her know I'll be a little bit late."

I didn't hear back from her even after we got off the train. By then it was five minutes before the meeting and we still had a few minutes' walk left. I just hopped on the Zoom, turned the mic and camera on, and popped my earbuds in. She didn't join until we were back in the apartment so it ended up working out.

I was expecting the woman that gave me the interview because she said she was one of the two advisors, but it was the other one. We greeted each other with good mornings, which I found a little funny since it was noon here now.

She asked about my desire for medicine, which ways I'm leaning, what courses I felt I struggled more in, which ones I felt I excelled in, where I lived, and how I liked my alma mater.

For courses, we settled on Anatomy and Sociology. My alma mater didn't offer Anatomy and at the JC when I was going through EMT then medic school, Anatomy was always one of the first courses to fill.

We looked over the medical schools that I'd put on my portal. The list had about 24 schools on it, most of them being in California. There were some MD schools, mostly DO schools. I had a couple schools listed in AZ, CO, and NM. I even threw in some Ivy Leagues and some schools in the Midwest for the hell of it.

"You have a really good list," she told me, eyeballing it some more. "The good thing about some of these is that if you get in, it's free but you have to be a physician in the area for some time."

At one point, it felt like she was kind of just sitting there and circling through a lot of the same things. "I'm sorry Cameron." We laughed. "It's just… you're my only student this year and that I've had in a while that's made it so easy for us." I made a shy expression, putting my face into my collarbone. "You know you did amazingly well in undergrad. Most people have to take all the courses you did either over again or for the first time so you've really got quite a wonderful foundation."

After going through everything and getting the spring courses planned–Intro to Microbiology and Developmental Bio–we started making a little small talk.

"You're not working today, are you?" she asked me with a sigh.

"No ma'am," I said, smirking. "I'm actually in Harlem right now with some friends from high school."

"Oh my God, that's so fun!" she cheered. "I'm so glad you've got some vacation time." She started asking me about NYU and Columbia and if I've seen their campuses.

"The very first time I came, I did check their campuses out and they're gorgeous. That's why I've got 'em on my list." We snickered.

"Yeah, you know, NYU would be perfect. It's one of those that will pay for your tuition if you're a doctor in New York for a couple of years. So…" she trailed. We had just talked about how one of the DO schools nearby would be great, especially since I would love to stay in CA. "…it would really be a wonderful school for you."

"I guess we'll just have to wait and see," I told her, feeling anxiety begin to bubble up.

We said our goodbyes and nice-to-meet-yous. Ending the call, I didn't really know how to feel. I was nervous, tired, and excited. Also, I was a little overwhelmed, but I knew I had so much to look forward to. So much was going right for me…so what the hell was wrong?

"How was it?" Asia asked, after muting herself.

"Pretty good," I told her, wiping my face. "I'm taking SOC and Anatomy starting January fifth."

"Exciting!" she cheered. "I'm so excited for you to be a student again."

"Yeah," I sighed. "I know I'm a good student. It's just… school, you know?"

"Trust me, I know," she giggled.

Xiomara was calling me. I almost missed it. We talked for a bit, then she let me go once she made it to her 11 am class. I opened *F That* right after hanging up and let the couple know that I was free. He sent the address. It was a 7 minute walk.

"I'm going to go for a walk for a little bit," I told her. "Get my steps in since I skipped the gym earlier."

"Have fun!"

Whether she suspected I was lying or not, she didn't let on.

Their place was in one of the public housing complexes that

was nearby. The guy met me in the lobby so he could bring me up. Once security waved us through after I showed them my ID, he led us upstairs.

He was *so* hot. He was a 6'3" pretty boy with short curly hair. His skin was glowing and he had a little five o'clock shadow on his jawline. He was wearing running shorts and a tank top and his muscles were MASSIVE. I genuinely couldn't stop staring.

He looked me up and down from across the elevator, smirking. "How's it been in the city?" His voice was very silky and masculine.

"Incredible," I sighed, marveling at the size of his quads. He snickered a little, folding his arms across his chest. Oh, this son of a bitch knew what he was doing. I wanted to bite the shit out of those veiny arms. I bet if I threw a 16 gauge needle into his arm, it'd slide in beautifully. "Are you guys just visiting, too?" My eyes didn't leave his nipples.

"Yeah, we're from Philly. We've just got a friend's place for the week while they're on a business trip."

We got to the 12th floor and walked out together. He punched a code into his door. It was a very cluttered one bedroom. It was small too. I could see his girlfriend lying on her side with her ass facing us from the door frame and my breath hitched.

I walked in, thinking he was behind me and introduced myself. She looked at me from over her shoulder. Her hair was also wavy but considerably darker than his, more black than brown.

She rolled to her other side and smiled.

"Hi," she peeped, waving her fingers at me. "Very nice of you to finally join us."

"Excuse me," he said from behind me. I jumped in place and let out a little bit of a scream. We laughed and I could feel my face go red as I apologized.

He set down the waters on the bedside table and beckoned me closer once he was sitting on the edge of the bed. His girlfriend was laying on her stomach now, watching the two of us. When I was close enough, he placed his hands on either side of my waist and started kissing my neck. I immediately let out a moan of relief and tilted my head back. I could feel every nerve ending in my body warm up to everything around me.

He did that for a bit. Then, I felt hands on my ass from behind and nimble fingers turning up the hem of my shirt to get it off me. He kissed my chest and nipples as they perked up at their touch. Her soft lips brushed against the middle of my back between my shoulder blades. Her fingers traced the muscles in my lats, sending chills throughout my back.

He patted the space next to him on the edge of the bed. She tied her hair up into a tight bun before getting on her knees and rubbing our thighs with her hands. "Be a good girl for Daddy and his friend," he ordered.

Her hands slid effortlessly up our thighs and into our shorts. We kissed each other as she used her hands to pleasure us. The shorts and underwear came off shortly after. He was more hung than *stallion* himself. Then, his girl got to work. He had one hand behind my head as we made out fiercely. Our tongues were exploring each other's mouths when I felt the tip of his girl's teeth reach the base of my pubic hair and her tongue coming out to lick my taint. I moaned into his mouth and squeezed her hand sprawled out on the sheet. She came up for air. A line of drool connected my crotch and her chin. She went down on her boyfriend with a little more difficulty but still succeeded. She went back and forth a bit between the two of us, using her hands on the one she wasn't actively giving head to.

When she got tired and took an extended break, she used both hands and took turns kissing us up and down. He took her hair gently in his hand and pulled her up to get her on the bed.

She pulled me to her gently. Once I was close enough, she straddled me and we made out. She pinned my hands down at my sides while she tormented me with her gyrating pelvis and neck bites. When she wasn't kissing me, he was while he stroked his massive dick covered in pre-cum and saliva. While we were kissing, he stopped to make a rotating motion with one finger. She put her pussy in my face. I immediately started tracing her with my tongue, closing my eyes to savor every last moment. I moaned into her as she took me back into her mouth and traced me from top to bottom.

"You love her tasty pussy, don't you baby?" he growled into my ear.

"Mhmm," I moaned, feeling her tighten on my tongue as she let out a whimper. I slowly inserted two fingers to feel the inside of her walls, making her whimper some more as she took a break for air.

When she took me back into her mouth, I felt her slobber reach my asshole. I locked my ankles together and squeezed her head with my thighs as I thrusted farther and farther into her throat.

"Fuck yeah," he moaned next to me. I peered at him. He was biting his lip and watching us intently, rubbing his nipples with his free hand.

I finally let go of her head after a few seconds of her struggling. She gagged loudly through her stream of incessant moans. Thankfully, nothing came up.

"*Fuck,*" she whimpered, her arms trembling as she tried to hold herself up. "*Fuck baby.*"

She played with me for a bit, her slobber lubing me up good. She kissed me up and down as she caught her breath. Her body was still shaking and writhing while I ate her out, using my fingers to open her up. Licking her slowly from clit to taint and applying light suction as I pulled away. My face was coated in her juices as I kept exploring her.

I slowed down a bit and focused on my breathing because I thought she was going to make me come. My legs began to bounce with light tremors. I was about to tell her to slow down when she started shifting. I kept my eyes closed to concentrate on my breathing and squeezing my pelvic floor so I wouldn't finish. I felt her take me deep again, this time with the bed rocking rhythmically back and forth. I opened my eyes to see him gently going back and forth into her. Most of his shaft was still not in all the way. His hand was placed at the small of her back as he talked her through taking his massive cock. Her eyes were rolling to the back of her head as he got farther and farther into her. He kissed her back and the back of her neck, burying himself into her, moaning loudly and telling her what a good girl she was.

There were so many instances where I almost came, but it was like she knew and was trying to edge me. I'd get to the precipice of a release and she'd take a break to breathe, gasping for air and pleading with ecstasy. Then, when I gained control of myself, I'd grab her hair and nudge her back to take me again.

He asked me to get on my knees like he was. She came up for air, gasping and gagging again. Her chin, neck, and chest were covered in her drool. She coughed into the bed as I oriented myself. Then, she took me into her throat again, holding herself up with hands planted in the bed as her arms trembled to keep herself up. He and I felt each other up and kissed with fervor while we both thrusted into her.

I lost track of time, but eventually his moans got louder and more frequent. He let go of my waist and rested both his arms across my shoulders as his eyes rolled to the back of his head. We leaned towards each other and he buried his face into my trap, kissing and nibbling it as he whimpered. His girlfriend's entire body was shaking beneath us and I could feel her throat vibrating as she cried out. I traced his back up and down with the tips of my fingers as he moaned and kept plunging into her. With one last plunge, one hand on the small of her back, the other gripping my left shoulder with his face buried into my trap, his body trembled while he growled on release. I twitched in her throat. Fuck, I was getting close.

He pulled out with a cross between a huff, a laugh, and a moan. Sweat was pouring off his face. I didn't think it was possible for his muscles to look any bigger but they did. She slowed down and let herself breathe for a sec. Her face plopped onto the bed, her ass still sticking up in the air. She whimpered and panted.

"Fuck," she moaned.

"Are you getting close?" He asked, reaching for his bottle.

I moaned as she started using her hands again, trying to milk me like a cow. I nodded and threw my head back against the head board. He threw protection at me.

"I think you've earned it," he told me. She looked up at me with all of it in her throat and mouth, bubbles forming at the base. "She's not gonna say no."

That worried me for a second but when I got into position, her ass arched and her face plopped onto the bed. He kneeled down off the edge of the bed, looking right into her eyes as she waited for me to start. She taunted me with a shake of her hips. I spit on her and teased her with my tongue for several minutes. She was trembling by the time that I was ready to fuck her. I did it slowly at first, feeling her walls part like the Red Sea to make room for me. She gripped the sheets and her walls held onto me as I started going in and out at a steady pace. Before I knew it, my own legs were shaking. My breathing grew ragged as I felt myself losing control. I kissed her neck and back, wrapping one arm around her to squeeze one of her breasts as I kept plowing, her moans getting higher and higher in pitch. I immediately felt my vision grow dark on the edges. I collapsed onto her with a shaking pant, still kissing her neck as the ecstasy faded away. My legs and arms still jumped a little bit. I was lightheaded as fuck.

"Did you like that baby girl?" He asked her, leaning in to kiss her sweaty forehead.

She nodded with a whine. "So good baby." She rolled over onto her back so she could face me. "That was to you by the way."

We laughed. I kissed her. "Thank you." He and I kissed each other, craning our necks above her. Then, we both sat and kissed her neck and cheeks, sharing her mouth occasionally. "This was the hottest sex I've ever had."

We snickered softly together. When I started getting up, they got up too. They kissed me goodbye and gave me a goodbye spank, watching and following as I made my way to the door. We kissed again before the door finally closed.

I turned, feeling elated like never before. "Holy fuck," I laughed to myself. Under my breath I added, "That was hot as FUCK."

It was 4:30. Showtime was at 7:30 so we still had plenty of time. Asia had texted asking if I wanted to go anywhere for lunch.

I made it to the apartment after she let me in. "Hey, did you see my text?"

"Yeah," I told her, still short of breath from the whole experience. "Just let me shower real quick, yeah?"

"Sure thing," she said, smirking at me from her chair. "I'm done with meetings, just working on my thesis a little bit. I'm ahead so we can go right after you're done."

The hot shower felt amazing on my fatigued and sore muscles. I was a lot sweatier than I'd thought. The middle of my shirt's chest and most of its back, especially at my shoulder blades, was damp with sweat.

Stepping out, I realized that I forgot my change of clothes. They were in the duffel bag, on the pullout couch I'd been sleeping on…behind Asia, who'd never so much as seen me wearing a V-neck. I wrapped the towel around my waist and walked out slowly, feeling a little awkward with my wet and washed hair sticking to my forehead. She saw me round the hallway corner and immediately put a hand over her mouth and tried not to laugh. She looked away awkwardly.

"Sorry," I snickered, sitting on the edge of the pull out and digging for underwear and socks.

"It's okay!" she shrieked, giggling into her arms with her head down. "Now would be a horrible time for Red to surprise us."

I threw my head back and laughed. "You think he'd be into it?" I bit my tongue in a cheeky grin.

"Oh shut up!" She laughed.

I grabbed all my things and waddled back to the bathroom, using the clothes to cover my chest.

We grabbed a quick bite off a Halal cart then made our way to a boba shop nearby. I got another chicken gyro and she got lamb over a rice dish. After that, we decided to go exploring down at Hudson Yard. We took the 1 to Times Square and decided to walk the rest of the way down. She said it was a gorgeous walk down anyway, especially at sunset.

Right she was, Times Square was one of my favorite places. The first time I'd ever seen it at night, I was getting out of *The Book of Mormon*. I was starstruck. It was gorgeous and exciting during the day, but it was magical at night.

We got some really good pictures of the sunset, the skyscrapers, people, cars, and the decorations. I also got a few candids of Asia, smiling and being cute.

I looked around at everything once we reached Hudson Yard. It was a little overwhelming, but it was so breathtaking. I'd never been this far down in Manhattan on foot. I'm sure that I would've loved it on my own but having Asia with me made it so much more special.

We finished our drinks so that we could enter the Vessel, a big beehive looking structure that glowed blue and shimmered orange and gold. Like the skyscrapers nearby, it was dizzying to be close and look all the way up at.

"Have you been up here yet?" I asked her, nudging her with my elbow and still contemplating the huge edifice.

"No," she admitted, shaking her head. "I've never wanted to go alone and Red is afraid of heights."

That made me laugh. "You're joking."

She snickered, shaking her head. "He gets really dizzy just walking by skyscrapers. I'm surprised he got on that Ferris wheel with us."

"Awww, *pobrecito.*"

By now, the sun was really low in the sky, barely peeking over the horizon in the distance. We got our tickets and climbed the beehive to see the sunset. While climbing, I started to get dizzy and had to hold onto the railings that they had. We took breaks and took different pictures on the different platforms, most of them coming out blue.

We made it to the very top, panting and a little sweaty despite the chill of the air. The city lay beneath us, scintillating in the fading sunlight and decorations from across the street. I walked to the nearest railing and looked down through the mesh that was there to prevent suicides. I knew my family would love to be here to see this.

I looked over to see Asia standing there next to me. I got scared for a half second then calmed as I saw her and we laughed at my fright. Just below us was the water between Jersey and Manhattan. The water glowed with the lights from below, busy as ever as ships docked and undocked.

"You okay?" she asked me, suddenly. "You kinda have resting bitch face most of the time so it's hard to tell—" we snickered as I slugged her shoulder playfully with a mocking scoff, "—but you look a little . . . pre-occupied."

I let out a really long sigh, not wanting to cry but already feeling like I would eventually. "I really don't know Asia. You guys have been really great, I promise…" I huffed. "This whole time though… I've just felt like…" I stared at the glowing lights below. "Like something is missing… I've felt like that for…" Shit, how long had it been? I wondered. "…a couple of years now, honestly. No matter what I do."

She gave me a sad look. "I felt like that for a long time, too," she trailed. She closed her eyes and took a deep breath. "Especially after my aunt died, you know?"

My heart broke for her. I remembered hearing about her aunt's diagnosis when I was a junior in college in the beginning of 2020 just before the shutdown. By the time everything opened back up again, she'd died. It was coming up on four years that she'd been gone. "Asia," I cooed, extending an arm out to wrap around her. She leaned into the hug.

"I mean, I know it's been over three years since she's died, but…" her voice caught, "sometimes it feels like it was just yesterday, you know?" She wiped a tear from her eye and sniffed quickly. "I'm sorry. I don't mean to make this about me. This week's supposed to be for you and–"

"Hey," I protested, hugging her a little tighter. "Don't do that, you guys have been amazing this week. You always are."

She went quiet for a bit. "When I was little, she used to take me and my siblings everywhere. She used to love places like this… with really pretty views." We went silent for a bit. "It's like…" she sighed, "…I have so much fun out here and see beautiful things everyday… and sometimes I really want her to be here with me."

That was it. That's what I'd been feeling all week, what I'd been seeking for long before this vacation. "I've been feeling that way a lot this week," I confessed. Tears welled in my eyes. I cleared my throat before I continued. "Mainly when I've been with you and Red—you guys have been great, trust me, it's just… I want what I have with you and Red with…" I choked on my words as tears started rolling down my face.

"Mmm," she cooed sadly, squeezing me a little harder. "I know they want the same thing with you, Cam."

The ache in my chest was back. "Part of me feels like I don't deserve it," I mumbled through tears, fighting a trembling lip. "Like I haven't been good enough for them." That I hadn't tried the way that I should. I was always so wrapped up in school and work. I felt guilty for not being there for them the way I felt like I needed to be. The way that I really wanted to be.

I don't think Asia really knew what to say. We just stood there in each other's arms until I stopped crying.

"You've been so great to Red and I," she reassured me. "I'm sure if you're half as good to your family as you are to us… then you are more than enough."

I sniffed and let out a small bout of giggles. "I don't deserve you or Red," I muttered. "Not really, anyway."

"Oh, stop it," she gave a harsh laugh. "Yes, you do." I was going to argue, but she started talking again. "You're not alone in feeling that way, you know? Oftentimes, I don't feel like I deserve Red. I didn't feel like I deserved him for so long… what had *I* done in my insignificant, banal, and mundane life…. to deserve a man who loves me as selflessly as he does?" A smile tugged on her lips. "He's the one who told me to apply to this program, you know? I didn't even think I was going to get an interview and when I did, I truly thought that the admissions team *surely* wasn't going to like me." We scoffed at the same time. "And now here I am, I guess."

"You're so coooooollll," I told her, shaking her a little again.

She rolled her eyes and nudged me playfully. "I'd kill to be half as cool and confident as you are."

"Asia, shut up, you're gonna make me cry again," I joked, but feeling my eyes actually well up. We snickered a little and she apologized.

We stood there in each other's arms for a bit and then a horrid gust of wind came through and she said she'd had enough of that. We laughed on our way back down the stairs.

"The show starts in an hour and a half, so we have about an hour to run around here at the mall," she told me.

It was gorgeous inside. The entrance felt very much like Valley Fair back at home, but then the layouts and looks mellowed out a bit. The prices however, did not. So many things that Asia and I thought were cute we immediately noped and walked back out. She did mosey around a stationary store that was pretty cheap, almost like a Daiso but a little more fancy. She ended up not buying anything because she didn't want Red to have to bring even more stationary to San Jose eventually. We took some pictures and then headed to the show once we had enough of being disappointed by disgusting ass prices on clothes.

We made it back with just a few minutes until the show started. It wasn't super crowded which was nice. In this smaller theater, I think a larger audience would've made me a little claustrophobic.

The show was… *indescribably AMAZING*. The cute Black girl that played young Alicia looked a lot like her. The mother had a powerhouse of a voice, my personal favorite in the show. The show incorporated Alicia's classics like *Girl on Fire, If I Ain't*

Got You, Empire State of Mind (which ended the show), and *No One*. Oh, that last one made me cry. The context for the song was heartbreaking. *LORD*, I was not okay.

It was the longest standing ovation that I'd ever witnessed when it was over. I'd only ever seen two other shows, but still. We walked out together, clinging to each other for warmth. She suggested a really good empanada place down the street so we went there to eat. Best empanadas I'd ever eaten.

We were back at the apartment by 11. I was exhausted. She looked pretty beat herself. We changed and brushed our teeth.

"Did you want to watch anything before bed?" she asked me, after spitting her toothpaste out.

"Honestly, I'm pretty beat," I admitted. "I'm probably just going to head to sleep."

Just as I was lying down and throwing the blanket over me, my phone started buzzing with Xiomara's phone call. I knew it wasn't late on the west coast and it really wasn't out here either, but I wondered why she didn't have anything better to do. I hated declining her calls, especially since I knew how sensitive she was. I just didn't want her to contribute further to all the noise in my head so I just let it ring. The vibrations of the next two calls lulled me to sleep.

November 4th, 2025, Day 6 In The City

I woke up feeling really foggy, foggy and *famished*. I threw one of the meal prep plates into the microwave and ate it at the table. I had a few text messages from Xiomara, mostly her wondering if everything was okay and apologizing for being such a pest. I rolled my eyes and shook my head with a smile, reassuring her that it was fine, that I was just extremely tired last night and didn't really have the bandwidth for a phone call. She apologized again and said she was just so excited to live vicariously through me because she hadn't come to the city since she was a little girl. I just heart reacted to her messages because I didn't really know what else to say.

I brushed my teeth and left for the gym. Muscle Mami–Teresa–was there. I'd been expecting her and it was nice to see her again. She came up while I was adjusting the weights on a curling machine. We side-hugged and chatted in between sets. She told me about the stress of her classes, the holidays, all the things her daughter wanted for the holidays, and the struggles of being a co-parent with another Caribbean person.

I walked her home when we were done, to be a gentleman of course. She coaxed me in with a kiss and a playful ass grab. I followed her in. She jumped my bones as soon as the door closed and the neighbors could no longer see us. We danced our way to the bathroom, making out as we undressed each other and got the shower ready. Once the water was adjusted to the right temperature for my back, I pushed her towards the back, trailed my kisses from her lips, down to her neck, across her chest, down her belly, inhaled the scent of her womanhood at her pubes, and ate her out. I had one hand on her ass, pulling her closer to my eager tongue and lips. The other explored the curve of her breasts, circling her areolas gently as I inhaled her scent. She ran one hand through the hair on the back of my head, tugging periodically or clenching her fists as my fingers started to explore the walls of her pulsing sex. Pulling away with light suction every time I stopped to admire its beauty, she would whine and pull my head back towards her, begging me not to stop. We locked eyes as I looked up at her while her body started trembling, one hand on the wall to keep her balance. Her walls locked my fingers in place as she came on my face and I licked up every last drop. Her taste and smell made me ravenous. She half laughed and half pleaded as I licked her all over, unable to get enough of her, her knees buckling as she took fistfuls of my hair and tugged.

We washed each other's bodies. After the soap had cleared, I couldn't help but finger her from behind, spreading her lips open with two fingers and rubbing her clit. My arms wrapped around her waist, leaning down a little to kiss her neck, traps, and shoulders from behind. She took my hand that was squeezing her breast and brought my fingers into her mouth, sucking on them. I reached into the back of her throat, making her gag and yelp as my other fingers reached into her hungry pussy. Her walls clamped down on me again as she moaned loudly. She practically collapsed onto me as she came again.

Feeling pretty good about myself, we shut the water off and made our way to her bed.

"Ow," I winced with a small laugh, as my orgasm subsided. She had bitten me so hard, my lip bled a little. "Nasty girl." My lip stopped bleeding fairly quickly so we kept making out, my hands playing with both of her glutes.

"Fuck papi," she sighed, burying her face into my neck. My fingers traced the back of her curves gently. "You treat all your girls special like this, huh?" A laugh bubbled from my chest. She giggled.

We laid on our sides to easily face each other while we made out a little longer, my hand still playing with her ass and hers playing with my hair.

I looked at her and rubbed a thumb across her cheek with a forehead kiss. *"Vas a estar en mis sueños esta noche princesa."*

She smiled at me and gave me a kiss on the forehead back. We kissed each other a couple more times before putting our clothes back on and kissing on the way to the door. She fixed my hair a little bit and then sent me on my way. My chest warmed as I left. She was so hot and so sweet. And I was *NOT* going to ruminate on this and let myself catch feelings for a stranger, but she was beautiful and the time I had with her was special. I truly wished her well.

Asia opened the door for me, hair still a bit messy from sleep. "How was the gym?" she asked, sitting back at the kitchen table, smiling a little.

"Pretty good," I told her, massaging my sore pec. "Got a good pump in."

She smirked at me and gave me a knowing glance. I was about to ask what she was smirking at me for. Then, she tapped a finger on the side of her neck, just to the side of her laryngeal cartilage. I panicked and shot a hand to the side of my neck. She broke out into a fit of giggles. "I was totally fucking with you by the way."

My face flushed red and hot. I was so embarrassed. I covered my mouth as I laughed, shaking my head and flipping her off. "Fuck you Asia." I grabbed a change of clothes and went to rinse off in the shower.

After we laughed a little more about it, we decided to go get lunch at an Italian place nearby. She just needed a little more time to work on her thesis for the day. I sat at the table and relaxed, checking messages and scrolling through the apps. Some hot people but nothing that would realistically work out today or that could really even have me over. Lots of pictures of torsos, penises, vaginas, breasts, and asses. A lot of them saved for later–with permission of course.

The Italian place was down by where she used to live. They had a gorgeous little seating area and a beautiful bathroom. It was painted black and had flowers etched on the black rimmed mirror. I ended up getting a $12 Rigatoni Bolognese, which is hard to beat. Asia got spaghetti and meatballs. The food wasn't as good as the Italian food we had in the Bronx (Chicken Scarpano) but it was still great–especially for the price.

"Did you by any chance want to watch the Bruce Springsteen movie later?" she asked me, twirling spaghetti on her fork.

I nodded, my mouth full of the bolognese. I swallowed. "I don't know shit about that man, but I love me some Jeremy Allen White."

We chatted about how her thesis was going. After we were done, we went to get milk tea at a nearby store a few streets up. Then, we started walking through Central Park. Central Park in the spring was gorgeous but in the fall, Central Park was jaw dropping, especially around the bodies of water.

Asia and I started reminiscing about all the stupid shit that we used to do in high school. Like when Red and I used to draw laughing faces next to every 69th page label on any textbook we could get our hands on or when I'd caught Asia and Red kissing for the very first time. The one time when we were 20 and they went for a closed-eye kiss and I playfully bonked their foreheads together. When I introduced the two of them to my very first boyfriend a few years back, Red told him that *he* was actually the first man that I'd ever loved.

By the time we were at the end of the park, the sun was at its lowest place in the sky before it set. I also really had to pee. We rushed into a Whole Foods to go. I nearly pissed myself too.

The next showtime for the movie was in about a half hour so we made our way into Union Square. I paid for her ticket since mine was free with my Regal unlimited subscription. We were some of the only people in the auditorium.

The movie was cute. It was a little slow in the beginning, but it sets a good foundation that it's going to be a movie about trauma. Spoilers ahead: there's a scene where Bruce Springsteen is having a flashback to when he was little. His father came home drunk and started demanding that he and his son start practicing throwing jabs. He was roughing him up and he was making the kid cry. It made me think of my own childhood. My father wasn't drunk, well usually he wasn't when he would do stuff like that, but he used to make me learn how to fight. He stopped eventually, but I hated every minute of it. There was another scene towards the end of the movie when Bruce finally decides to go to therapy. In his first session, he just starts bawling. I did just that. In fact, I cried non-stop for three sessions straight. So there was that.

We left the theater, both feeling a little sad. I wrapped my arm around her shoulder. She wrapped hers around my waist. "It's just a sad boy season, isn't it?" I joked as we left which made her laugh.

We made our way to Times Square for the A train up to 125th. We decided to eat again so we got Subway because she said she'd never had it before–which was absolutely fucking crazy. We split a footlong breakfast sandwich with egg and cheese since it was the cheapest, even more so than the meal of the day. Walking through the streets, we took some more pictures of each other and of the city, making each other laugh and telling each other how cute we were.

We made it into the apartment by midnight. We finished our food pretty quickly. After asking her how it was, she said it was surprisingly good. I threw my napkin at her playfully and revealed it was my go-to when working in Merced because it's one of the cheapest options.

"Last night in New Yooooorrrkkkk," she sang. I nodded with her. The week had gone by way too fast. "How do you feel?"

"Sad that I'm going back to a mundane life," I admitted with no hesitation. She smiled and laughed sadly with me. I rolled my eyes to not make a big deal of it. "I am looking forward to my future. It's just a little boring right now."

"That's better," she laughed, squeezing my hand over the table.

We stood up and hugged each other, rocking each other back and forth.

"God, I love you so much girlie," I huffed into her hair, rubbing her back.

Patting my back, she replied, "I love you too Cam."

November 5th, 2025, Day 6.5 In The City

I woke up around 9. My flight was at 11:50 so I had a decent amount of time. I rushed breakfast, another microwaved Jimmy Dean croissant and showered quickly. When I got out, Asia was up and getting dressed. She helped me get my things together, mainly handing me things that she noticed I'd left behind so I *wouldn't* do so.

It was almost 10 by the time we hobbled out to the street corner for the M106 to La Guardia. We counted everything that I was supposed to have on me. All the clothes, my wallet, my cell phone, my car keys in the bag, shampoo, conditioner, and loofah, my chargers, and the gifts that I bought while I was out here.

We stood there shaking like chihuahuas in the windchill. Once the bus came, we hugged again, squeezing each other tight like it would be years before we saw each other again. We waved until we couldn't see each other through the windows anymore.

By the time I got to my gate, everyone had already boarded. I checked the time. We still had another 15 minutes to take off.

"Are you Cameron?" they asked as I approached. I nodded. "Come on through."

I watched the skyline grow smaller and smaller as we ascended into clear skies. We were technically still in New York after a few minutes. I already wanted the plane to turn back.

November 5th, 2025, A Few Hrs After The City

We touched down in San Jose just before 7 pm. I tried to sleep, but I was too restless. I grabbed a snack downstairs at the baggage claim, since I hadn't eaten in damn near 12 hours, once I grabbed my duffel bag.

Xiomara called me when I was getting back into my car after taking the shuttle back to the parking garage. I declined her call and started the engine. I went to the Valero nearby so I could get gas and an energy drink for the ride. I didn't want to fall asleep at the wheel. I needed to get home in one piece. I had my family counting on me. I had a community to care for.

I was zooming through the 101 South, halfway through with my energy drink when my vision started tunneling. My mind began racing with memories from my childhood. I was lying in bed with Luke, trying to put him to sleep as he cried for our parents who were out working late. I was crying in my own bed after Mom and Dad told me to stop being stupid. They told me I was just a hormonal teenager who wanted to fuck anything with a pulse. I was 17 years old and lying in bed with a man and woman *decades* older than me. They'd been so impressed by how mature I was for my age. They took turns with me, laughing at how easy it was to make me finish. I was 15, lying in my new bed in Merced. I hated everything about this new life, there was nothing for me to look forward to here. *What was the point of doing anything anymore?* I sat year after year alone with Luke at home on the holidays as Mom and Dad tried to pull in holiday pay. All the eye-rolls, all the dishes slammed into the sink, and all the hugs cut short because my parents asked the most intrusive questions about my relationships and social life.

My ears rang painfully. I could feel my heart beating against my rib cage, desperate for escape. My chest started to ache. I couldn't even take deep breaths to calm myself. Every inhale was a hot blade into my lungs and I let out a cry for help.

I lost control of my wheel. And I blacked out.

November 9th, 2025, Day 4 After The City

I was standing outside of the behavioral health center in the area. I had my bags and was waiting on my ride. I called for help that night. Crying on the side of the road, I told the dispatcher it felt like I was going to die, that I couldn't make the thoughts stop racing. I couldn't stop the flashbacks of memories that tormented me. I knew that I had everything going for me and wanted to do so much more with my life, but I was a hollow empty shell of an individual and that it felt like I didn't deserve anything the world had to offer me, no matter what I did.

Santa Clara County EMS brought me into Valley Med with *supra-ventricular tachycardia* (bad fast rhythm that left untreated can become a lethal rhythm) with aberrancy. I was given adenosine in the hospital and monitored for the night. Then, they took me to the behavioral section where I awaited placement. Thankfully, it was pretty fast.

Xiomara called me. "Hey you," I answered.

"The bet is off," she told me.

I snickered a little. "Dude, I totally forgot about that."

"Would you have won?" she asked. It sounded like she was crying.

"Just the fifteen," I told her. "Hey, are you okay?"

"As okay as someone whose good friend just had a three day grippy sock vacation can be."

I rolled my eyes. "I'm okay Xiomara." Silence. "Really, I am." We talked a little longer. "Hey, I gotta let you go. Some family members just pulled up to bring me home."

Asia and Red pulled up in her mom's electric KIA. They smiled sadly at me. Red was out first, nearly jogging to me and scooping me up into a hug. I let my bags down and wrapped my arms around him tightly. Asia came up next to join our hug. She cried into my chest and he cried into my hair. They told me they were so happy that I was okay and that they couldn't bear the thought of losing someone else they loved. I was sad about having them worried. My new meds made crying (and coming) a little more difficult.

We grabbed a late lunch at the iHop downtown. I had to take my food to go because my eyes were bigger than my stomach, but I did manage a few bites on the way to Merced. They drove me. We'd always planned on them coming to see me in Merced. Now we had the opportunity, albeit a bit macabre. I pointed that out to make a joke and they hated how funny it was, rolling their eyes. We only needed to stop once in Manteca to charge the vehicle for about a half hour. We dicked around at the Target. Red and I used pool noodles to have light saber fights, making noises and everything. Asia disapproved or at least pretended like she did. She was recording us and rolling her eyes.

We got to Merced and my parents' place a little after 5. My dad was already waiting for us outside the complex by the gate. We laughed at him, rolling our windows down to say hi. It'd been a few years since they'd seen my dad.

"My baby is home!" he cheered, lifting both hands above his head and attempting a jog, even though he needed his rickety ass cane for balance.

They parked in guest parking. When I got out, I could hear the pitter patter of Bailey's paws as she ran to me. I knelt down and let her attack me. She was a flurry of kisses, scratches for attention, and yelps of affection. I scratched her all over and held her head in place once she settled down a bit to kiss her head, right in between her ears. Asia and Red played with her too, having only ever seen her on video or in pictures.

Mom was limping her way towards us with her arms wide open for a hug and there were tears in her eyes. She cried a little when she hugged me. "My baby." I kissed her on the cheek and let her go inside ahead of us.

My dad had dinner ready. Luke, Daniela, and the baby were

there too. Luke hugged me for a really long time, fighting a tremor in his hands as he squeezed me and they handed the baby to me. She immediately started acting shy, trying to look at her shoulder and avoid eye contact. Asia and Red were so happy to finally get to see her. Red and Luke dapped each other up, never having met but hearing a lot about the other. Luke thanked him for everything that he'd done for me. Luke told Asia it was nice to see her again and pulled her in for a hug.

We ate Dad's food. My Dad told jokes about me from when I was a little kid and Asia and Red told their stories of their own. Luke, the little shit, put me on blast a couple of times with stories about smoking weed together and taking him to clubs before he was 21. Asia and Red looked at me like they didn't know who I was, mouths agape. All I could do was shrug and shovel the menudo into my mouth.

My parents insisted on hugging them both as they got ready to leave, thanking them profusely for everything. They told them how glad they were that I had friends like them and that sometimes they worry that I don't have friends and over-occupy my life with school and work too much.

"Okay, yeah Dad," I insisted with a laugh. "Let them leave."

They said their goodbyes again as I walked them out. We squeezed each other in a final embrace before they got back in the car.

"Take care of yourself Cameron," Asia pleaded with a sad smile. "Please don't hesitate to call us if you ever need us."

"I won't," I promised. I meant it. "See you later, huh?"

They left the complex with a final goodbye and wave. Red sniffed and rubbed his left eye as he drove away.

November 14th, 2025 9 Days After The City

I quit my job that morning. Everybody was asking me why and telling me not to make any rash decisions, but I was burnt out. A lot of my anxieties were coming from being in a field that I had lost passion for quite a long time ago and maybe never had to begin with.

Work gave me an extended medical leave so I could take a proper break away from everything. That morning, I woke up on the couch at my parents' place. I made them breakfast. I put on a jacket and some jeans. I grabbed the letter that I wrote the night before and I went to work to talk to Ventura, hoping to catch him before the full swing of things kept him too occupied.

As I walked in through the garage in the back, the overnight cleaning crew was finally packing their things up for the night. The *corridos* were still bumping, best believe it.

Some of the other crew members were happy to see me. A few came up to hug me and told me they were glad that I was doing better. One thing that I wasn't going to miss about this place—how word spread like brush fire.

I caught Ventura stepping into the supervisors' office and called for him as he fiddled with his keys. He looked over his shoulder at me with a mixed expression of both relief to see me and confusion about what I was doing here.

"Hey!" he greeted. He opened the door. "C'mon in."

It was welcoming and warm inside. He took a seat behind his desk. I grabbed a chair and sat it in front of him. He started his monitor and his coffee maker.

"Glad to see that you're doing a lot better Mancía," he told me, fixing his attention to me and clasping his hands together. "To what do I owe the pleasure of you coming to see me on a day off?"

I gave him a sad smile as I reached into my jacket pocket on the inside. I'd folded it into thirds so it would fit. When he saw it, his face sagged a little. Sadness and confusion flickered in his eyes.

"I'm quitting." I unfolded the paper and placed it on his desk. His jaw hung open as he searched for the words with the letter in one hand.

"I don't understand..." he murmured. "I'm sorry, but... you know, you've built so much here..."

"I've *loved* working in healthcare," I reassured him. "And I've loved my time in EMS." I could feel the emotion rising in my chest. I cleared my throat and locked eyes with him. He finally put the letter down. "I just know that this isn't the place for me any longer and I have to do what's right for me and my family, at least in the moment."

He nodded slowly. The gears were clicking into place. He'd come into the acceptance phase of this pretty quickly. "I know this wasn't an easy decision for you to make."

I gave a harsh laugh with a shake of my head. My eyes welled up with tears as I looked at him. "Part of the reason that I hung on for so long was you." His head tilted to the side. "Not in a bad way," I laughed, a tear falling. I quickly wiped it away. "Your mentorship and… how great of a friend you've always been to me. You really opened up doors for me in a way that I can never truly thank you for." His own eyes were starting to get foggy behind his glasses. I sniffed. "I never wanted to disappoint you, you know? You're like the only person whose opinion of me really matters."

We both snickered at that. He took off his glasses and rubbed his face with both hands for a few seconds.

He shook his head at me. "Nothing you have ever done has disappointed me." I bit the inside of my lip to stop myself from crying. "I have *always* marveled at your bravery, your integrity, how in tune you are with yourself and those you love, and how much love you have for them and humanity as a whole." He wagged a finger at me. "I have always been *so proud* of you and who you've become in the last four and a half years."

Once he made his way to my side of the desk, we hugged each other.

"Let me know if you ever need anything," he told me as I stepped away after a bit. "I'm always just a phone call away."

I shifted awkwardly. "You still know the hiring director for the ER Tech position at base hospital?"

He let out a soft chuckle. "I'll call 'em right now. Let 'em know you're more suited for the in-hospital setting."

*****

After all that, Dad and I finally got to watch the Bruce Springsteen movie together. I told Mom she was invited too. It would've been really nice to have her. She said she wasn't very up for it, but that she wanted to come over later and watch movies at my place and I agreed. She'd only ever been to my apartment twice before. I told them both that we should have more movie nights together at my place, as a family. They both agreed.

Dad and I were driving to pick up Mom. The car had sustained minimal damage on the side of the road after I'd lost control of the wheel. It only suffered a ding on the front bumper that was only really noticeable if you squinted. Luke brought my car back from the tow parking lot a few days ago.

There was music playing from my liked songs playlist. My dad reached for the knob to turn it down. "I'm really sorry that I used to do that to you Cameron."

I knew what he meant. I glanced at him quickly. I took his hand in mine. "It's okay Dad, I forgot all about that."

"No, it's not okay," he insisted. "That's why I stopped doing it." He sighed. "I wanted you to learn how to fight… so that you could protect yourself from bad people. Growing up, I didn't have anyone to protect me." He swallowed. "And the people who were supposed to be protecting me were the ones hurting me the most." Rage coursed through me, my knuckles turning white on the steering wheel. "We weren't beating your ass… so we thought we were doing a pretty good job, you know?"

I didn't argue with him. He wasn't wrong. "I promise I'm okay Dad."

He nodded slowly. "You don't have to tell me anything that you don't want to…" he started. "…but I've hoped and prayed that nobody's hurt you like your mother and I have."

I swallowed the lump in my throat. Then, I told him everything. I told him about the men and women who groomed me in my late teens. I told him about the men who forced and/or coerced themselves into me when I had made it clear that I didn't want them to. I told him about the time that I woke up after blacking out drunk to someone going down on me in a dark room, how I hated myself for a long time for finishing, even though I was being assaulted by a stranger.

"Please don't blame yourself, okay?" I pleaded, swallowing the lump in my throat, my voice breaking. "There's nothing either of us could have done. Some people are just . . . really fucking shitty."

We both fell silent for several moments. Neither one of us knew what else to say–*if* there was anything else *to* say. "I'm really sorry that that happened to you." Silent tears streaked his face. "You didn't deserve any of that."

I wiped the tear from my cheek. "I know." I scoffed and sniffed.

As we pulled onto our street, he started talking again. "I'm sorry that everything turned out the way that it did," my dad sighed. "I worked so hard… to give us everything that we wanted and it all just turned to shit."

I laced my fingers through his over the console. "I know you tried," I told him. "That's all that I care about."

My dad chuckled sardonically, smacking his knee with his other hand. "I knew I raised you right." He gazed at me admirably. "We're going to be alright though. Isn't that right?"

"Yes Dad," I agreed, kissing the back of his hand in mine. *No One* by Alicia Keys started playing. "I love you. You know that, right?"

He gave a curt nod. "I love you too Cameron."

About the Author

Isaac Grijalva is a bisexual and queer Latino from San Jose, California who works as an EMT by day. He is the oldest brother of two boys and an uncle. Isaac attended the University of California, Merced and matriculated in December of 2021 where he obtained his *B.S in Biological Sciences* and *B.A in Psychology.* Though Isaac's passion lies in medicine and he's working on going to medical school, it's been a life-long dream of his to publish at least one of his manuscripts. He has been writing since he was 10 years old and has many unpublished manuscripts in his Google Docs. When Isaac has free time, you can find him at the gym, walking his dog Bailey, taking friends or family members out to the movies or to eat, on a spontaneous day trip to the beach or the mountains for a hike, traveling to new cities, or sitting in the corner of a library/bookstore/coffee shop working on his next manuscript.

You can connect with me on:
- https://isaacgrijalvabooks.com